Pivotal Studies in the Global American Literary Imagination

Series Editors
Daniel T. O'Hara
Temple University
Philadelphia, PA, USA

Donald E. Pease
Department of English
Dartmouth College
Hanover, NH, USA

This series will present new critical perspectives on the histories and legacies shaping the divergent visions of America in the world within literary texts. Texts that re-envision America and its relationship to the larger world, in ways other than exceptionalist, will provide a point of critical focus for these cutting edge scholarly studies. Using the unique format of Palgrave Pivot to make an incisive intervention into current scholarship, the stress in these books will be on how American literary texts have and continue to contribute to the reformation of the vision of America in the world from roughly the antebellum period to the present. As "transnational" approaches to scholarly production have become mainstream, Pivotal Studies in the Global American Literary Imagination considers the complexities of such an appropriation and, instead, develop alternative global perspectives.

All American genealogies from the New England preeminence through the mid-century modern cold war consensus to post-modern dissensus, transatlantic, global/transnational turns (and counter-turns) would be tapped and the word "American" in the title will include all of North America. All critical perspectives would also be welcome, so long as the focus is on the question of how the texts and subjects discussed bear on the question of the global American literary imagination. Finally, the authors will demonstrate how to read their chosen texts, revealing the ways these new interpretations foster informed critique and revised critical methods.

Books published within this series should fall within the Pivot length limits of 25,000–50,000 words.

More information about this series at
http://www.palgrave.com/gp/series/15082

Gina Masucci MacKenzie

Maternal Representations in Twenty-First Century Broadway Musicals

Stage Mothers

palgrave
macmillan

Gina Masucci MacKenzie
Holy Family University
Philadelphia, PA, USA

Pivotal Studies in the Global American Literary Imagination
ISBN 978-3-030-32336-3   ISBN 978-3-030-32337-0   (eBook)
https://doi.org/10.1007/978-3-030-32337-0

This Palgrave Pivot imprint is published by the registered company Springer Nature
Switzerland AG
The registered company address is: Gewerbestrasse 11, 6330 Cham, Switzerland

To Isabella and Iris, my inspiration
To Dan, my mentor

CONTENTS

CHAPTER 1

Introduction

Abstract This chapter uses feminist theory to provide an original understanding of how musical theater could be, written by or for women, to demonstrate for audiences the range and scope of possibilities in the realm of motherhood. This book will show the current limits of the display of critical imagination on Broadway, in the portrayal of motherhood. The current Broadway musical climate ironically forecloses the possibilities of non-traditional ways of representing motherhood, by employing pre-Modern binary distinctions. The mother in the musical must be allowed to write herself, thus be allowed greater time on stage, especially through song. The new iterations should not follow a stereotype or script but should allow for the expression of all types of motherhood, both positive and negative, generative and subversive.

Keywords Feminist theory · Motherhood · Broadway · Abjection · Lack · Jouissance · Real · La langue

The Broadway stage of the twenty-first century has been one of great freedom. This freedom, both reflected in and directly inherited from London's West End, represents the pinnacle of the form of musical theatre. As an art, the musical is distinctly American, but since the musical's Golden Age, the pond has been easily crossed and this form has been shared and developed globally, with the West End and Broadway

© The Author(s) 2019
G. M. MacKenzie, *Maternal Representations in Twenty-First Century Broadway Musicals*, Pivotal Studies in the Global American Literary Imagination, https://doi.org/10.1007/978-3-030-32337-0_1

1

standing as its beacons. Broadway is the model for how the form grows and develops. The form of the musical has seen great changes. The strict two-act structure with overture and entr'acte are no longer expected by producer or audience. *Contact* made way for dance plays to be widely accepted, even heralded by mass audiences, partially because of the attraction of the woman in the yellow dress. *Contact*, which debuted on Broadway in 2000, gives the audiences three discrete stories to witness, mostly through choreography. *Movin' Out* quickly followed suit as a dance play devoted to the loosely based tales of growing up on Long Island in the Vietnam era. The form forgoes a well-drawn plot, eschews dialogue, and uses different performers to sing and dance the same role.

Musicals such as *The 25th Annual Putnam County Spelling Bee* experiment with form through the introduction of improvization and audience participation. In "*Spelling Bee*," audience members become an integral part of the plot, obliterating the fourth wall. *If/Then* and *Fun Home* experiment more with narrative form than theatrical form. *If/Then*, a 2014 musical starring Idina Menzel, fresh from *Frozen* success, simultaneously tells the story of one woman, Elizabeth, and the two paths that her life could take, so that the audience, with the protagonist, exists in both realities at once. *Fun Home* uses three actresses to play the same character in three different stages of her life. The narrative trajectory and the actresses move in a seamless, somewhat nonlinear path through the play, with no intermission or division of acts. To varying degrees, audience has accepted these musicals and their new formats.

Along with form or structure, twenty-first-century musical theater sounds different. Lloyd Weber's *Jesus Christ Superstar* was a rock opera extraordinaire debuting on Broadway in 1971, merging popular and theatre music. Audiences were meant to feel at ease with the sound, as if it was part of their daily soundtrack. Sondheim's usage of minor keys and extensive recitative had the opposite effect, alienating the audience in a somewhat Brechtian fashion. Still, both of these dominate composers used traditional musical form and instrumentation to convey their sounds and stories. Broadway musicals sound different now. Rock and pop are standard with the music of twentieth-century icons such as Billy Joel, Green Day, and Bruce Springsteen being only slightly modified. Pop composers such as Sting, Duncan Sheik, and Sara Bareilles have tackled the composition of entire scores, while *Rock of Ages*, among others, features popular rock music from a variety of artists. Along with rock, and pop, now not only common, but somewhat expected in commercial musicals, we hear hip-hop, rap, country music, Latin rhythms, and spirituals. *Hamilton* remains the most wildly successful merger of musical styles and has made hip-hop standard Broadway fare.

Despite these recent changes in musical theatre form and sound, little has been done to advance or experiment with character portrayals on Broadway, especially those of mothers and mother figures. It is important to understand why that is and what, if anything can or should be done to change that.

The options for female characters, particularly mothers, in all narrative forms, are ones of constant critical inquiry. Rachel Blau Duplessis's *Writing Beyond the Ending*, published in 1985, remains of the best studies of women writers and characters in the twentieth century. Duplessis's work represented a radically new conceptual framework for understanding women writers and the potential they give to their characters. While the figures and texts she uses do not focus on drama or musical theatre, her strategy can easily be applied to any narrative text. The core of her argument is that women writers, especially contemporary women writers, see through binary distinctions and give their female characters more options than those traditionally allotted to women in literature. Her book ironically begins, "Once upon a time, the end, the rightful end, of women in novels was social – successful courtship, marriage – or judgmental of her sexual and social failure – death. These are both resolutions of romance. Sometimes, the ends of novels were inspirational, sublimating the desire for achievement into a future generation, an end for female quest that was not fully limited to marriage or death" (Duplessis 1). The options offered to women were not many: marriage, death, or maybe, a future legacy not to be enjoyed by the woman in the moment. This is a worldview in which deferment seems to be the most freeing option. Such deferment of gratification can only serve to make larger and more demanding the process of establishing that which will allow future fulfillment. At best, that deferment creates anxiety for the woman, which she will never see, sated. At worst, it forces her to put forth effort with no satisfaction. This is the Lacanian Real, par excellence, and while in theory, at least for Lacanian devotees, that Real is the best we can achieve in our lives, as it frees us from all social and psychological refuse, it is most definitely not practical. The Real is a state of ultimate solipsism and a complete break with society. While in theory, this is appealing, in practical application, it leads to psychosis. What is needed and what Duplessis implicitly hopes and demonstrates is that women authors can give practical paths as examples for women, beyond societal conventions, that are not Real or psychotic. Those paths will not always be enjoyable or stable, but they will give greater range of opportunity.

Duplessis explains, "As a narrative pattern, the romance plot muffles the main female character, represses quest, valorizes heterosexual as opposed to homosexual ties, incorporates individuals within couples as a sign of their person and narrative success" (5). This is frequently what musical theatre, even great musical theatre, does. *Guys and Dolls* (1950) ends with a double wedding; Sara's and Adelaide's dreams of marrying and reforming low-level criminals come true. Uncle Abernathy even sings, "More I couldn't wish ya, / than to wish you find your love / your own true love/ today." His wish is for the happy ending to her romance. Loesser gives it to the audience, and the audience loves it. The neat conventional ending makes the audience feel at ease. The goal is met; the romance is resolved.

Even musicals that are considered innovative or edgy resolve themselves in ways that reflect Duplessis's criteria. Jonathan Larson's *Rent* is generally considered to have ushered in a new wave of musical theatre that appeals to a younger, hipper demographic than Broadway was entertaining at the end of the twentieth century. An updated version of Puccini's *La Boheme, Rent*, is the story of a loosely related group of artists and their associates suffering through poverty, addiction, and the AIDS epidemic. Throughout the first act, Rodger and Mimi have an on-again/off-again "romantic" relationship that devolves because of her drug use and his lack of willingness to disclose his AIDS diagnosis. When finally on the verge of death, Mimi and Rodger reunite. While Rodger's successful courtship of Mimi and her death are intimately related, co-dependent, in fact, they fulfill both of the outcomes Duplessis describes: successful courtship and social death. What at first glance appears to be one of the most innovative musicals of the end of the twentieth century is not. That is not to say that it is not a great work; it is simply not as atypical as we think.

Next to Normal, the brutally honest 2009 Broadway musical about a mother whose son's death and bipolar disorder led her to walk away from her husband and daughter gives us a glimpse of possibilities different from those Duplessis sets out. A contemporary riff on Nora Helmer, Diana Goodman struggles as she approaches her Real though her bipolar disorder and, at some points, actively resists treatment for her delusions, as those delusions bring her in touch with her dead son. By the end of the musical, Diana chooses to leave her family, to stay with her parents. Her choice eschews romantic and societal convention and in that denial of convention she is hopeful. The audience is left disconcerted though; Diana is a mother who chooses to leave her child, not for the sake of her child, but for her own good. The decision is still considered selfish, and although Diana is presented as hopeful at the end of the play, the audience relates more to her bewildered family. Audiences are not ready for a woman who makes choices that thwart societal norms.

Helene Cixous's seminal essay, "The Laugh of the Medusa," provides a mechanism, albeit an extreme one, to write innovative portrayals of women, especially mother figures, on stage. While Cixous does not specifically write about theatre, she does not target, nor exclude any genre. In the first sentence of this essay, she asserts, "I shall speak about women's writing; about *what it will do*" (2039). When written in 1976, Cixous knew that the women's writing for which she was advocating had been millennia in the making and would not be accomplished easily. Her essential argument, in its blunt and then radical assertion, is that "… woman must write woman" (2041), meaning that no man can write a woman's body or, in turn, a woman character. Cixous's argument is that a woman must write her body; she makes the connection between a woman writing and a woman masturbating, both creative endeavors designed first to bring pleasure to the self, with little care for the effect the act might have on others. Masturbation, a secret pleasure, can come into the open when it is sublimated through the new body of a text. Cixous claims, "[B]y writing her self, woman will return to the body which has been more than confiscated from her, which has been turned into the uncanny stranger on display – the ailing or dead figure, which so often turns out to be the nasty companion, the cause and location of inhibitions. Censor the body and you censor breath and speech at the same time" (2043). Writing is a radical act of self-assertion and an act that allows a woman to claim her whole self. Although Cixous does not go this far, writing, as she describes, is an anti-Cartesian act of rejoining the mind and body.

It is not just writing itself that could enact Cixous's anti-Cartesian stance, but other forms of art, especially musical theater, as it is able to connect multiple art forms: writing, music, performance, into one presentation. Purposefully, the term "unified" is excluded here, because what slips away is as important as what comes together. Musical theater, even as it brings together multiple art forms, is not a unifying art.

The struggle that some audiences have with accepting the form is that it does not often hold together in the way the audience wants it to. It is not "normal" for people to sing in the middle of an intense argument or even in the rain. Audiences perceive that lack of normalcy and that lack is the lynchpin in unification. In moving from Cixous's perspective into those of Kristeva and Lacan, that slippage is the defining nodule of the art form itself and is also its most honest and female point. It is where the combination of art forms is exposed that it offers its greatest power and its greatest parallel with womanhood.

It is not just the mind and body of a woman herself that is brought together through writing, but also that of her child. Unlike Winnicott, Klein, Kristeva, and so many others in the psychoanalytic tradition who explore the dynamics of the mother/child dyad, and who assert, in varying ways, that motherhood produces a fraught, even contentious relationship between the mother and child, and the mother and her own body, Cixous seems to oppose that. Her image of motherhood is intensely positive. She writes about motherhood, "I don't mean the overbearing, clutchy 'mother' but, rather, what touches you, the equivoice that affects you, fills your breast with an urge to come to language and launches your force; the rhythm that laughs you; the intimate recipient who makes all metaphors possible and desirable ... In women there is always more or less of the mother who makes everything all right, who nourishes, and who stand up against separation; a force that will not be cut off but will knock the wind out of the codes" (2045). The impetus of motherhood, that which brings a woman to want to bear a child and that which touches the child in a positive, generative fashion, is also the drive to create narrative. The ability to conceive and bear children is also the ability to conceive and bear text. Cixous does not draw significant distinction. It is not, then the product, but the process that is important here and the choice that the woman has to partake in the process. If woman must partake in the writing process to enact the generative powers of writing the body, then to see a greater range of women characters, particularly mothers on stage, there needs to be more women writers whose work is acknowledged. This is not frequently the case.

In the twenty-first century, still very few women write or direct for the Broadway musical stage, with a few significant exceptions. Susan Stroman dominated the first ten years of this millennium, creating *Contact* in 2000 and directing *The Producers* (2001) and *The Scottsboro Boys* revival (2010). Jeanine Tesori's music gives sound to *Caroline*, *or Change* (2004), *Shrek, the Musical* (2008), and *Fun Home* (2015). Without Kristen Anderson Lopez's contributions to the music and lyrics of *Frozen*, both on screen and the Broadway stage (2017), the sound track of every pre-school birthday party would be much different. Each of these women and others, such as Quiara Alegria Hudes, Heather Hatch, Nell Benjamin, Lisa Lambert, and Lisa Kron, have made immeasurable contributions to the theatre arts. To a decent degree, these women have received profession honors and even for a few, fleeting public recognition. Interestingly though, many of the productions these women have helped to write and stage do not offer the kind of freedom for female characters, especially mother figures, that the stage needs to present. While *Caroline, or Change* gives a glimpse at what a substitute mother figure can contribute, and *Fun Home* shows how an absent mother can give a daughter both great freedom and confusion, these two shows, and several others, certainly do no show the range of potential mother characters.

Julia Kristeva's work, particularly "Stabat Mater" and *Powers of Horror*, offers interesting perspectives on motherhood that might provide avenues for creating and staging various images of motherhood. One key concept in Kristeva's understanding of motherhood is abjection, the process through which a subject rids herself of all physical and psychological mater that keeps her locked in tandem with another person, particularly a child. Kristeva writes, from the perspective of the subject, "'I' want none of that element, sign of their desire; 'I' do not want to listen, 'I' do not assimilate it, 'I' expel it" (*Powers of Horror*, 3). The process of abjection is the key to the subject giving birth to herself. This subject can be either the child, taking control of her own life and asserting herself apart from the domination of her mother figure, or can be the mother, giving ridding herself of the weight of motherhood as defined by the other. As Kristeva again writes in the subject's voice, "My body extricates itself, as being alive, from that border. Such wastes drop so that I might live, until, from loss to loss, nothing remains in me and my entire body falls beyond the limit … " (*Powers of Horror*, 3). The physical processes implicated here, crying, vomiting, urination, defecation, and sexual release, allow the subject to extricate herself, from the physical and psychical material weighing her down. These most base functions of the body take the subject out of herself and her relational entanglements. They allow her to focus on herself as self, as she disengages to allow herself freedom to define herself, not through others, but alone.

The tangible aspects of this process are important as related to the-atre. Theatre is a living art, a physical form of expression. The body of the mother or child, which Kristeva describes, can also easily be the body of the actor. After all, many actors too engage in a process like abjec-tion when they prepare for a role. To assume the role of another, an actor must rid herself of herself. While the mechanisms for enacting this purge are different depending on the acting school or practice an actor espouses, the similarities exist. To be another person on stage means that an actor consciously is not oneself. Preparation for stage is then a perfor-mance of abjection.

This makes identity itself an imprecise concept. Identity, for neither actor, nor character, is not fixed, due in part to the process of abjection, a process that Kristeva herself links with ambiguity. The ambiguity of the process and the position of the person abjecting herself are that of the subject. There is no object in that process; the goal is of the self and for the self. Without an object, the process becomes intensely solitary, so if applied to a mother/child dyad, abjection is disentanglement. It is a "... *precondition of narcissism*" (*Powers of Horror*, 13). In "Stabat Mater," Kristeva also explains that the mother/child dyad is "... an idealization of primary narcissism" (1). Such narcissism, though, is frowned upon by current society, which still romanticizes the position of motherhood. While Duplessis categorizes the limited roles of women in narrative, Kristeva does so with mother figures. She explains there are "... two fun-damental subcategories of Western love, courtly love, and the love of the child" ("Stabat Mater," 136). In courtly love, the woman is beheld and idealized by the man from a distance, loved by and through metaphor, not physicality. The woman's sexual being and desire are foreclosed. With the love of a child, the mother is clung too, but her physical needs still denied in favor of those of her child. Her motherhood comes at the cost of her narcissism, the result of her abjection, the process through which she can become herself.

Instead, the child is more likely the subject who can use abjection to her benefit, as it is one of the most profound "... attempts to release the hold of *maternal* entity even before ex-isting outside of her..." (*Powers of Horror*, 13). While the process of abjection can assume different paths for different subjects, it commonly follows a pattern of prohibition or elimination of a substance or object, foreclosing the possibility of the mother giving or passing something along to the child or expulsion, in which an object or substance is violently pushed away. In both of those common paths, the object expelled or denied is then, in some way, purified and made into an artistic or religious experience.

If contemporary commercial musical theatre is missing its full range of mother figures, it is, in part, due to the over-purification of the abject. To purify is to make the abject into art, but to over-purify is to polish away the sublime identity that is necessary for honest artistic expression. To give a closely related example from theatre, Williams purifies his life experiences into art while writing *The Glass Menagerie*. He polishes away the abject in writing *Vieux Carre*. Both works draw heavily on Williams's autobiography, but only the former is able to purge a specific set of life experiences, Williams' interactions with his mentally ill sister and hone in on the experiences, to rarify them into art. Its tight structure and distant tone help it to avoid becoming cloying and overly sentimental. *Vieux Carre*, on the other hand, exploits Williams' experiences as a young homosexual writer in New Orleans and turns them into a melodramatic parade of pitiable characters in an overblown rift on *La Boheme*. Turning the abject into art presents enormous challenges for the purging artist as it requires simultaneous intimacy and critical distance.

Just as Kristeva explains that, the abject is ambiguous and without object, she also writes, "[F]or the sublime has no object either" (*Powers of Horror*, 12). If both the abject and the sublime are intensely and solely subjective experiences, then they cannot be commodified or even replicated, which presents an enormous difficulty when trying to present that experience though theatre, an art which begs not to be purified, but which is, and whose level of purification is, frequently related to the amount of commercial time and money being used to stage that production. Here in lies deep irony and an obstacle to giving the commercial stage a more well-rounded presentation of mother figures in musical theatre.

Because the intensity or innovation of a production is mitigated by the financial investment, current productions often limit their character's potential scope. Instead, the abject is usually staged in what Kristeva identifies as its narcissistic contradiction. She claims that narcissism gives a glimpse of the abject either through its near omnipotence, or through its lapse (*Powers of Horror*, 15). This leads to the staging of two nearly stereotypical mother figures, the overbearing mother or the absent mother. Both allow the child access to the process of abjection, but only engage with that process in an expected or conventional way. Neither is very successful at giving the mother access to the abject process though, locking the mother into a limited pattern of options. Musical theatre needs to do better.

And it can. Musical theatre has potential that many other art forms do not, because it is inherently self-contradictory and fractured. The musical itself is comprised of multiple art forms competing with each other in the same space. One art form is musical's book, the basic plot, and dialogue of the story. Another is the music combined with the song and dance numbers which intrude upon the book, masquerading as part of it, but not actually incorporated, despite all attempts by contemporary musical theatre composers to create integrated and through-composed musicals. The attempt to integrate book and musical is not for naught. The attempt strengthens the performance by bringing the song and story closer together, but they are never really one. In the conclusion of *The Musical as Drama*, Scott McMillian writes, "One wonders if a good musical penetrates human perplexity and misery because what seems to be triviality becomes a complex opening of private matters into the gaiety of the numbers" (197). Moving from McMillian's theory, song gives a safe place for abjection to begin. "Last Midnight" from Sondheim's *Into the Woods* provides an interesting place for analysis of this.

In this song, the Witch, Rapunzel's mother, who drives the narrative, is faced with enormous grief from the death of the daughter. At the end of Act 1, she transformed from ugly witch into beautiful enchantress. Now the grieving witness too much death, filled with self-blame, the Witch enacts what seems to be a process of reverse abjection, calling upon her powers and those of her mother, to change her back to an ugly witch. Instead of ridding herself of the "warts and hunch" that a person might want to eliminate, to make herself more attractive or comfortable, she requests those things back. She wants to take back the abject material that reminds her of herself when her daughter was alive. From the Witch's perspective, abjection leads to separate from her status and a mother and without a mother, her daughter died too. In this case, the abjection is presented as a failure because the mother's real desire was not to separate from the child. The will to reverse the process is the will to negate the separation. While a profoundly interesting character, with an outstanding score to sing, the Witch is a stereotypical mother figure, and while her final number is not light-hearted, its dramatic effect, ending in her explosive disappearance from stage, privileges spectacle over story reinforcing the idea that the song is less meaningful than book.

Critics usually affiliate the book with the complexity of good drama: character development, plot structure, and theme. The songs are relegated to the status of fun set pieces, with the ability to add levity to the drama, or at least a respite from the seriousness of the dialogue. That perception, however, is incorrect. The intrusion of song into book, regardless of lyric content or harmonic structure, creates a rift in the expected; such injection of the unexpected is the heart of what Brecht defined as "the alienation effect." Brecht's intention was for the audience to sense the disjointedness and therefore establish a critical distance between itself and the events onstage. It was a distinctly anti-Aristotelian move, designed to bring theatre, particularly musical theatre out of the realm of chorus cuties and escapism, into serious political and social discussions. What Brecht missed is that musical theatre is never simply chorus cuties and escapism, but is always, because of its ability to straddle at least two art forms (without taking into account dance or visual components) a serious, political act. It defies the law of genre, and in its defiance, sometimes, done with tongue-in-cheek jazz hands, it echoes the position of the mother herself, as she is the figure, in society and psychoanalysis, frequently placed outside the realm of the law.

With both the genre of musical theatre and figure of the mother being outside the law, the figure of the mother becomes doubly complicated in the musical itself. First, though, it is important to understand how the mother is the figure outside the law. Genevieve Morel's recent book, *The Law of the Mother*, reexamines the mother figure in light of Lacanian psychoanalytic theory, to explain how the mother, as she who is always beyond the law, is related to her own jouissance and to the jouissance of the child. It is, in particular, this aspect of the maternal relationship that is not staged in its fullest complexity and that, I would argue, needs to be explored in much greater depth.

Stemming directly from Lacan, parental roles, most commonly, but not exclusively bound by sex, are divided as the Name-of-the-Father, or the law-giving, Symbolic, patriarchal order, and the "Desire of the Mother" or that which is marked only by absence, and desire of the child for the mother to return, combined with a curiosity about what was so enticing as to take the mother away from the child. This leads to two types of maternal figures: the absence and the over-present. As Morel states, "The signifier of the desire of the mother, *signifier of an absence*, which would become a lack, needs to be distinguished from these maternal worlds which have the force of law, and which rather testify to an *excess of presence*, as in the case of the mother who commits infanticide" (16). While Morel, drawing on Lacanian references does mean literal infanticide, symbolic infanticide is nearly as important and far more common. Such a state would involve the mother rendering the child, of either sex, impotent. It would mean locking the child into the realm of the maternal with no ability to create one's own symptom or key to jouissance. As Morel reminds her readers about Lacan, "[I]n the Seminar *RSI*, the definition of the symptom as 'the way each of us gains jouissance from the unconscious in so far as the unconscious determines him' (88) is the mechanism through which an individual creates her own marker, her own piece of the real. When that unconscious is determined by the mother, who is unable to separate from the child, then the symptom is not really that of the child, but that of the mother incorporated in the unconscious, unconsciously." We might here imagine the negative image of Cronus. Instead of the father swallowing his progeny, only to expel them later at the command of the one who had not been consumed, we can envision the mother, embracing her child so tightly to smother out of the child, any ability to think or feel for itself. To be free, the child cannot wait for another to come along as savior; instead, the child must escape of its own accord, less like Cronus and more like.

The opposite maternal reaction could also be true and just as detrimental. Instead of consumption, the mother could seek to expel the child from the beginning. This image is not to be confused with that of the abject processes Kristeva described, but is one in which the mother refused the child access from birth, so that the child, held at arms' length always, has no access to the desire of the mother and cannot begin a process of letting go herself, because she has been let go of too soon.

Ultimately, the mother/child, particularly mother/daughter relationship, is a struggle to the death of one or the other. If the daughter fails to assert her own subjectivity over that of her mother, she is subsumed back into the mother and becomes herself abject material. To return to the stereotypical dichotomies of female characterization, she is the whore, the conglomeration of negatively received forces and actions shunned by society, whereas, if the mother fails to assert herself, she takes on the role of the Madonna, the ever faithful, ever serving virgin who cannot assert her own subjectivity as she sacrifices that for the subjectivity of the other. There is little room for freedom or variation. Women are either Momma Rose or Gypsy. There has to be more, and there is, but those options right now are very infrequent.

Attention to mother/child relationships on the Broadway stage in the twenty-first century can be divided into three basic categories: absent, overbearing, and inconsequential. The absent mother is one who is noticeably absent from the stage altogether or absent as a significant presence in the lives of other characters or even as an agent in her own life. Those musicals include: *Next To Normal, Spring Awakening*, and *Wicked, and Billy Eliot*. In each of these commercially successful plays, the mother figure, through her absence in the lives of her children, is shown as being the cause of their negative actions. In Wicked, the implication is that had Nessa Rose's mother lived, Nessa Rose would not have been evil, and that had her extramarital dalliance not occurred, Elphaba would not have been born, a desirable non-outcome for her immediate family. Here, when the mother was present, her actions were reprehensible and when she is dead, her missing presence is the cause of evil. This presents an impossible situation for the character and reflects the impossible situations of many audience members. The perceived absence or intellectual immorality of Melchior's mother in *Spring Awakening* is blamed, in the musical, for his moral demise. The mother in *Next to Normal*, while one of the most complicated maternal figures in musical history, is emotionally absent to her daughter, leaving that daughter in a state of confusion, anger, and ironic hyper-focus. In *The Color Purple*, Celie, as the mother figure, is present, but her children, because of circumstances beyond her control, are absent for most of the play. Each of these examples will advance the concept that commercial Broadway remains comfortable with the stereotype of the mother figure as the moral compass for her family. When that compass is absence in any way, the child's ethical behavior is also compromised. The chapter will explore the ways in which this presentation is actually progressive, as it subverts the convention in drama and literary tradition that the father is guiding figure of the family. Instead of the absent mother, what is needed are new representations of motherhood that remove this moral burden, giving both mother figures and their children more individual autonomy and independence.

The figure of the overbearing mother, a convention of musical theatre, with *Gypsy* as the example par excellence, is explored. While this category is possibly, the most anticipated and exploited to be explored in this text, it is also a necessary exploration into the ways in which common stereotypes intersect with feminist literary theory. The mother who abandons la langue, or who is too mired in it, will overwhelm the child. We see this in the fantasized mother/son relationship in *Next to Normal* as a mechanism for coping with her perception of her failure as a mother. This reaction formation can be read as a failed attempt at ecriture feminine. *Matilda* and *The 25th Annual Putnam County Spelling Bee* are comedic examples of the overbearing mother figure, whose children give voice to their detrimental presence. Through them, the audience sees the figure as one-dimensional while this chapter seeks to explore the multi-faceted components of these characters. *Spring Awakening* also offers this figure to audiences in the form of Wendla's mother, whose strict conservatism leads to her daughter's lack of knowledge and eventual death in the guise of maternal protection.

It is in the figure of the inconsequential mother that Broadway characterization can find the greatest freedom. In this figure, there is an expectation that mother figures will play a larger role in the actual stage performance than they do. Such incongruity of expectation and presentation not only challenges audiences' expectations, but also demonstrates some movement in changing conventions. These barely-there mother figures, while sometimes simply a product of plot and stage convention, are also significant in the potential they could possess or the lack they leave in character and audience through their minimal, but intriguing presence. In *Passing Strange*, the mother figure, present and negative at the musical's opening, gradually diminishes in importance or in the protagonist's perception of her lasting importance, rendering her, superficially but increasingly inconsequential. Parents, particularly mothers, are barely present in *The 25th Annual Putnam County Spelling Bee*, and when they are mentioned, never staged are virtually irrelevant. For only one character/competitor, is her mother relevant in her life, in a negative fashion? In *Fun Home*, audiences are confronted with an interesting inconsequential mother in this genre. While Allison's mother is a consistently present and strong supporting character in her own right, the role she plays in her daughter's life is noticeably secondary to that of her relationship with her father. While the plot of the musical necessitates highlighting that father/daughter relationship, and because the musical is autobiographical, there are limitations to the way in which Bechdel can manipulate the story, the self-contained performance demonstrates the outcome of mother figure whose role in the ensemble of her daughter's life has had a detrimental effect. The truth of this portrayal does not fetishize or fantasize the role of the mother. Instead, it presents an accurate alternative to the polarized presentations audiences usually expect. *Dear Evan Hansen* also explores the role of the inconsequential mother, as the grieving mother is presented as having been so out of touch with her son, that she has no idea what is true or not regarding his actual life.

The tragic but accurate commentary of the role of the mother in the average teenager's life has been popularized by *Thirteen Reasons Why*, the book and Netflix series that shares many themes with *Dear Evan Hansen*. While it is easy for audiences to lament or to blame this type of mother figure, really, this figure is the one who offers the greatest freedom from convention, as neither she, nor her children are forced into stereotype.

What is ultimately needed is a New Mother, a figure who denies and defies the present categories.

CHAPTER 2

The Missing Mother

Abstract This chapter examines examples in which the mother figure is absent in the lives of other characters or even as an agent in her own life. Those musicals include: *Next to Normal, Spring Awakening,* and *Wicked,* and *Billy Eliot.* In each of these successful plays, the mother figure, through her absence in the lives of her children, is shown as being the cause of their negative actions. This chapter advances the concept that commercial Broadway remains comfortable with the stereotype of the mother figure as the moral compass for her family but when that compass is absent in any way, the child's ethical behavior is also compromised. The chapter will propose that what is needed are new presentations of motherhood that remove this moral burden.

Keywords Absent · Abjection · Transitional object · Jouissance

In the history of the Broadway musical, productions with significant roles for mother figures, or explorations of mother/child relationships are noticeably missing until the postwar Golden Age of musical theatre in the 1950s. Prior to that, the focus of Broadway narrative was on romance with some outstanding experiments with political satire. While the dramatic stage was producing works with brutal family dynamics and mother/child struggles by the era's best playwrights: Williams, O'Neil,

© The Author(s) 2019   17
G. M. MacKenzie, *Maternal Representations in Twenty-First Century Broadway Musicals,* Pivotal Studies in the Global American Literary Imagination, https://doi.org/10.1007/978-3-030-32337-0_2

Miller, and Hellman, to list just a few, the musical stage was just beginning to explore family dynamics, and even so, those explorations were infrequent.

Oklahoma gives audiences the character of Aunt Eller a stereotypical matriarch and substitute mother. In this, the first musical driven by the narrative, not the song, dance, or spectacle, the mother figure is not the innovative character. The form itself, combined with the iconoclastic antagonist and ballet innovation, combines to revolutionize musical theatre.

From there, musical theatre audiences of the Golden Age met *The King and I's* Anna, *The Sound of Music's* Maria, *Gypsy's* Mamma Rose, and *Bye-Bye Birdie's* Mrs. Peterson. Leaving aside Mamma Rose, these mother figures adhere to a type. Rogers and Hammerstein's *The King and I*, from 1951, is the story of Anna, a schoolmistress, brought to Siam during the height of British colonization, to education the King's children, and ostensibly to help Westernize the country. Her involvement with the king's children is superficial at best; the real foci of the musical are the relationships between Anna and the king and the over-arching cultural clash. Anna is more cultural mother than actual mother (Kantor and Maslon, 2010). Anna is, at best, a substitute mother figure, whose role as such is underdeveloped.

In 1959, Rogers and Hammerstein stage what might be their most popular musical *The Sound of Music*. It is the story of a young woman, Maria, who is pulled from her convent's noviciate, to act as a governess for the seven children of an Austrian military captain whose wife has died. Once there, she acts as the substitute mother, turned stepmother, who reforms the house and nearly absent father, while Nazi invasion of Austria. Again, the relationships among Maria and the children are superficial at best. Only with Liesl does Maria have any individual interaction or influence. Liesl, the oldest Von Trapp child is in love with Rolf, a young man who turns to the Nazi party and eventually turns in the Von Trapp family as they are fleeing Austria. As Liesl learns of Rolf's increasing betrayal, Maria acts as a confidant and friend. She is a loving and supportive advocate for them. She brings joy and music to their home. She is sugary sweet and while she is the protagonist, she is not the focus of the musical. Fighting against the horror of Nazi Germany is the real theme of the musical, with the individual human characters there to give life and bring empathy to an issue no other composers/lyrists would bring to the musical stage. *The Sound of*

Music is remarkable, in its political timeliness, just not for its treatment of mother/child relationships.

The end of the Golden Age sees *Bye-Bye Birdie* debut in 1963, another musical which hovers about important societal issues: the draft, the dissolution of the American family, ethnic prejudice, but those issues are treated with such distance and gentle humor that those concerns lose their potency. Instead, it becomes a story of teenage crushes and pop idols. Albert Peterson and his secretary, Rosie, together act as songwriter and publicist for Conrad Birdie, an Elvis-type, about to be drafted. Albert and Rosie, in love, want to leave the company so Albert can pursue his dreams of teaching English and Rosie can be housewife. Albert's mother is adamantly and dramatically opposed. At first unwilling to defy his domineering mother, Albert gains confidence and asserts his own desires to gain personal and romantic freedom. Mrs. Peterson's overbearing nature is stereotypical and the audience never gains nuanced insight into her motivations, all negated by Albert's happy ending. Taking a cue from its most famous song, everything in the show is designed to "Put on a Happy Face," without delving into character psychology.

The only musical of the Golden Age which presents a uniquely complex mother figure is *Gypsy*, which remains one of the strongest examples of complex mother/daughter relationships in musical theatre. Gypsy, which debuted on the Broadway stage in 1959, is the vaguely autobiographical story of burlesque performer Gypsy Rose Lee. Her fraught relationship with her mother Rose, the show's real protagonist, begins in her childhood, as her mother subjects her and her sister to the endless grind of the vaudeville circuit. Louise, later to become Gypsy Rose Lee, is the younger daughter, the backup to her more talented and beautiful sister, June. Both daughters have well-drawn and nuanced relationships with their overbearing mother, to be discussed more fully later, as this musical was revived for the Broadway stage in 2008.

The sparse history of mothers on the musical stage continues mostly with absent or nearly absent mother figures. Mothers in *Sweeney Todd, Annie, The Phantom of the Opera*, and *Les Miserables* are notably missing; family dynamics of any kind were still not common functions of plot or character development. In *Sweeney Todd*, Mrs. Lovett does function as a mother figure for Tobias, but Johanna is motherless. From infancy, she is a ward of the judge who had imprisoned her father. Kept in an asylum, a Rapunzel-like figure, Johanna is easily swayed by the men around her and looks for them to save her, as her mechanism of escape.

Even the show's love song, "Johanna" includes the lyric, "I'll steal you, Johanna / I'll steal you ..." (Sondheim, 1979). This is not a reciprocal love; it is a bastardized version of courtly love, with the night, admiring from afar, but not content to worship from a distance. This knight, or more accurate to the plot, sailor, wants to get as close as possible. The crafting of that lyric shows that Johanna is to be "stolen," absconded with, not of her own accord, but of his desire. There is not mother figure to protect her or to show her that she can assert herself or her own will. The mother's absence leads to a lack of self-possession in the daughter. This pattern does not hold true for the effect maternal absence usually has on daughter figures. It is, in fact, quite the opposite. Usually, the absent mother makes the daughter plucky and strong-willed.

While *Annie* is by no means a work of storytelling greatness, it does present a motherless daughter, whose status as an orphan has shaped her into a self-assured, resilient child. Annie is a character whose motherless status has left her by age eleven with the desire to escape and find something better for herself. It is at her unceremonious return to the orphanage after running away, that she encounters Grace, Mr. Warbucks' secretary searching for a child to bring home for the holidays. Coincidence predicated by Annie's self-mothering leads to her permanent change in life situation. For her, an absent mother was a gift; it necessitated her sassy spirit and allowed her to put into place the mechanisms and events that lead to her gaining a father in Warbucks, a substitute mother in Grace, and more money than any child, especially in the depression, could comprehend. It is a fairytale ending for a fairytale start.

The fairytale start nearly always includes the death of a mother which leads to a tragically impoverished or abusive situation for the child. These are the circumstances at the beginning of *Les Miserables* for Fontine, a factory worker/prostitute and her daughter Cosette, who she has entrusted to the care of the Tenardiers, the sinister innkeeper couple who have douped her. Fontine is mother absent by necessity. She longs to be a part of her daughter's life; she sacrifices her physical and psychological well-being to earn her daughter's keep. Her inherent goodness is recognized by Jean Valjean, who attempts to save her job and her life. In lieu of that, he instead is able to rescue her daughter and raise her as his own, in relative wealth and comfort. For Cosette, while her mother is physically absent from her daily life, Fontine is a quintessentially good mother; she sacrifices her entire life for her daughter's well-being. She is the fantasy of what every mother is supposed to be. Originally published in 1862 France, Victor Hugo's *Les Miserables* is basically a melodrama, set at the beginning of the French Revolution. It's melodramatic plot that ends in romantic satisfaction for Cosette reinforces Duplessis's basic theory; women can either be dead, like Fontine, or in loving romantic relationships. Fontine is the sacrificial mother and Cosette the daughter who flourishes in her shadow. At the musical's ending, when Valjean is dying and Cosette learns the truth of her life, Fantine returns, a benevolent ghost, present to witness her daughter's transformation into womanhood, and to act an angelic mother figure for Valjean. She, with Eponine sings, "Take my hand, and lead me to salvation/ Take my love, for love is everlasting/ And remember the truth that once was spoken / To love another person is to see the face of God" (Kretzmer, 1987). She has transcended her role as Cosette's mother; she is heavenly mother. She will cradle Valjean in her arms, a French revolutionary version of the Pieta. She is, as Kristeva claims in "Stabat Mater," "...the *consecrated* (religious or secular) representation of femininity subsumed under maternity" (133). That image, so perfected and refined to fulfill societal expectations, leaves no room for either mother or daughter to assert a new path. Within the confines of the musical, neither wants to; each longs to uphold societal norms. These characters fit with stereotypical expectations for family dynamics being portrayed on the Broadway stage in *Les Miserables* original 1986–1987 debut season, but it was staged again in 2006/2007, and it is because of that revival that it is most interesting for consideration here.

Of course, for a revival, especially one that is already an adaptation of a famous novel, the possibility of re-envisioning a character is limited. There has to be some significant level of adherence to the original character, which is retained. Additionally, the original musical version was an enormous success, running from 1990 to 2003, a total of 6680 performances, a total only exceeded by *The Phantom of the Opera* and *Cats*. The musical was revived in late 2006 and ran until early 2008. Perhaps the musical's appeal had decreased, but a run of over a year, for a revival, is better than average for a Broadway musical. Little was changed from the Broadway original to the revival, and the most significant changes were those made to staging of ensemble scenes and technological upgrades. The mother characters, and their daughters, remained intact. The audience is presented with two mother/daughter pairs in Act 1, Fantine/Cosette and Madame Thenardier/Eponine. Fantine, struggling and dying to pay for her daughter's keep with the Thenardiers, who have promised to care for the child, sings, "I Dreamed a Dream" in which she acknowledges the fantasy of her relationship with her daughter's father. The song, filled with romantic longing and the recognition that her dream is shattered, does not at all focus on her dreams for her daughter, nor does it express a longing to be with the little girl. Because the audience never sees Fantine in the relationship about which she sings, the audience transfers the love about which she sings to her daughter as that is the vestige of the relationship visualized for the audience. Fantine does, in lesser moments, articulate her love for her daughter and her willingness to do anything to provide her with a good life, but that desire is not the desire of her only solo vocal number. Fantine's biggest moment on stage, the one for which she is remembered, one of the most iconic Broadway musical moments to date, has little to do with Fantine as a mother, but instead with Fantine as a jilted lover. That is her self-definition.

As a mother, she is absent. Fantine has given her daughter to the Thenardiers to care for with the naïve assumption that they will care for her as they do for their own daughter Eponine. As melodrama will have it, they do not. Cosette, a tiny Cinderella-like figure, is forced to be a slave in their inn, while their own daughter, Eponine, is treated as a princess. As luck and melodrama will have it, Eponine too will have a reversal of fortune and become the street waif. When the audience meets Cosette, it is she who sings about her absent mother in the heartbreaking "Castle on a Cloud." In the song, Cosette dreams of a life "so different from this hell she's living" (Kretzmer, 1987) and sings, "There is a lady all in white / She holds me and sings a lullaby / She's nice to see and she's soft to touch / She says, "Cosette, I love you very much" (Kretzmer, 1987). The mother image that Cosette envisions is the exact opposite of both her birth mother, Fantine, and her substitute mother, Madame Thenardier. She imagines her mother to be a virginal vision, more the ghost of Fantine presented at the end of the play to escort Valjean to heaven, than the dirty impoverished factory worker the audience sess. The audience is presented with both sides of the maternal stereotype: the virgin mother caressing her child, or the woman who, "… plays the virgin in the light, but needs no urging in the night" (Kretzmer, 1987) as Fantine is described by her wealthy assailant when she rejects him. Her options, just as Duplessis claims, are marriage or death. Since she has been "ruined" by her affair, her only option is death, which she handles with waifish grace, leaving her daughter

2 THE MISSING MOTHER 23

abandoned, but only temporarily, as Val Jean, her new father figure, and Fantine's non-sexual savior, steps into save the day, and rescue Cosette from the Thenardiers.

Fantine, absent first by giving her child to board with another couple, and then through death, is the ultimate sacrificial mother, setting up a dynamic of reversed power over the child. Instead of the absent mother having no control, as she is absent, the sacrificially absent mother gains more control as her saintly nature establishes her as a beacon of light and goodness to which the child is drawn and tries to emulate. In her mother's absence, Cosette is cloyingly good. When in the Thenardier's household, given the examples of thievery and deceit, Cosette remains dutiful and quiet. Ironically, she is the opposite of the mother she is trying to emulate, who will fight, emotionally and physically for her safety and security. In this case, with the mother absent, the struggle a daughter usually faces to establish her own separate identity is foreclosed upon before it starts, so the daughter has no mechanism for rebellion. She cannot begin the process of abjection which leads to self-identification, because, without the presence of the mother, the mother has no opportunity to project onto the daughter her own identity. Without that projection of mother onto daughter, there is not enough material in the daughter to abject, and without the process of abjection, there is only a weak process of self-creation. There is no fight; hence, Cosette, while given an excellent vocal line and the cute boy to marry, is one of the most flatly drawn heroines of the Broadway stage. To be blunt, she is boring, partially because the absence of her mother gave her no way to round out her character.

The question remains though, why do audiences still flock to this stock characterization of the mother/daughter dyad in the twenty-first century? The easy answer is, of course, that it is easy to handle. Audience members thrive on the theme and variation. The theme of the absent mother and motherless child is one all too familiar. That, combined with the socially acceptable positive outcome for the child, Cosette is raised in comfort by a father figure who adores her and marries the handsome revolutionary of her dreams, leaves little impetus to create characters that derive from the norm.

More significantly though, for the twenty-first-century Broadway theatregoer, the absent mother is representative for any lack that an audience member might feel, whether that lack is maternal, social, financial, psychological, etc. The missing mother, at the core, is an absence.

When the child, especially the daughter, can survive without that maternal presence, the audience members, guided to identify with the child, also feel that they can overcome any lack in their own lives. It is a simplistic form of transference, but it does not give enough variety of character or experience to satisfy an audience for very long. Commercially though, that is key. If an audience is not satisfied, they will come back, watch the same musical again, or see other musicals, to try to fill the lack.

In *Wicked,* which debuted on Broadway in 2003, the audience is also presented with an absent mother whose daughter tries to fill the void she has left, but here the young woman seeks to fill the lack via socially unacceptable means, which may or may not be more advantageous for her. *Wicked* is the backstory of *The Wizard of Oz.* Told mostly in flashback, just after Glinda has descended from her bubble to let her subjects know the Wicked Witch of the West is dead, it is the story of Glinda and Elphaba in their prep school days, learning wizardry and figuring out their romantic and social lives. While Glinda comes from an intact and adoring family, she is adorably vapid, motivated by her need to remain at the top of the social food chain. Elphaba is green, in every sense of the word, and is only at school to accompany her older sister, Nessarose, who is paralyzed. Elphaba is happy to be in her older sister's shadow, but cannot remain there, as she is the more talented wizard of the family and the one brave enough to challenge the injustice she sees increasing around her. There are many fascinating aspects concerning feminism and roles for woman on Broadway in *Wicked,* especially in regard to Elphaba. These themes are expertly explored in the *Changed for Good: A Feminist History of the Broadway Musical,* which pays special attention to *Wicked,* but which does not, in a sustained way, address the implications that Elphaba's mother has on her daughter's character.

Elphaba is the product of a drunken night that her mother spends with an unscrupulous elixir salesman. His potion, which she drinks before they consummate their relationship, is the implied reason, along with the adultery itself, that Elphaba, the product of the relationship, is green. This incident is most certainly a variation on the theme of the sins of the father, but here, taking cues from *A Doll's House,* it is the sins of the mother revisited on the child. This speaks volumes about the cultural implications and judgments surrounding motherhood. If a woman chooses a sexual partner, for pleasure, as she does in the musical, then she is to be damned with a child who does not meet society's expectations. The only socially acceptable thing to do then is to be absent from the child's life, but in grand ironic fashion, maternal absence doubly damns the already bastardized child. Elphaba, without her mother's influence, is first presented as sour, cranky, vaguely dangerous and unlikable. *Wicked*'s progressive move though, is that those very characteristics which make her, at first, the villain, ultimately posit her as the iconoclastic hero. As Wolf explains, *Wicked* and Elphaba develop nearly cult-like followings as women, disenfranchised for any number of reasons identify with her.

Partially because Elphaba does not have a mother present and active in her life, as presented to the audience, she is forced to assert her own ideas and not simply follow society's norms. There is a correlation, or not causation between Elphaba's absent mother and her ability to think critically on her own. She sees the injustices around her and wants to speak out against them, to change them. She will not tolerate the mistreatment of the "Animals" and is particularly upset when she witnesses their loss of speech. She despises the collusion between the Wizard and Madame Morrible and their attempts to co-opt her budding talent. She is comfortable being perceived as evil as long as she can accomplish actual good. All of this is because, since her mother is absent, she is able to develop a deep sense of autonomy and self-direction.

Only two characters potentially derail that self-assertion, Fiyero, her lover and Nessarose, her sister. When Nessarose, who is wheelchair-bound and corrupted by the power of being governor of Oz, faces unrequited love from Boq, Elphaba uses her power to enchant the shoes that allow Nessarose to walk, removing the obstacle of her physical disability, which is assumed to be the reason Boq does not find her attractive. That plan backfires, as Nessarose's inherent cruelty, not her physical disability, as made her unloveable. Elphaba then uses her magic again, after Nessarose has used magic badly, to remediate the situation, turning Boq into the Tinman. Instead of maternal loyalty, Elphaba has loyalty to her sister, and that loyalty causes her to act irresponsibly. The message is then that female familial ties lead to drastic negative action. Elphaba has deep guilt and resentment over her actions on her sister's behalf and does not allow herself to be manipulated again. Her familial ties are broken, but she still cannot be her true self. Elphaba is a revolutionary, but she also wants to live her life with Fiyero and so to live, she, with Glinda fakes her death, and escapes. Elphaba is at her best when she lives her life on her terms, not defined by an other.

For much of Act 1, Elphaba is defined as the ultimate other. She is green, after all, because of her mother. That physical sign marks her as other from birth. When she arrives as Shiz, she is the other opposed to Galinda's bubbly obnoxiousness. When foisted upon each other as roommates, Elphaba and Galinda have immediate visceral reactions to each other. Galinda is every stereotypical and superficially perfect girl that Elphaba is not. "What is This Feeling?" encapsulates their differences and allows each woman to define herself in relief against the other. Elphaba, this early in Act 1, is not yet comfortable in her own skin. As Galinda decides to tutor Elphaba in the ways of stereotypical teenager girldom, Elphaba's confidence in her true self starts to grow. Galinda acts, in part, like a substitute mother.

Some critics, including most significantly, Stacy Ellen Wolf, the queer romantic overtones of the relationship between Galinda and Elphaba and this book does not want to deny those strains. Wolf's argument is grounded in lyrics and well-constructed. I want to assert that an audience can add another layer to that relationship. As in many romantic relationships, the model is the parent/child dyad. Here, Elphaba has no significant relationship with her mother and as a young woman, abject from birth, and seeking a way to self-identity, the first woman figure she encounters who wants to tutor her in the ways of being a woman holds both romantic and maternal attraction. At the root of the mother/daughter relationship is narcissism which also underlies the child's choice of future romantic object. Jacqueline Rose points out in *Mothers: An Essay on Love and Cruelty* that, "... it is the mother's sensuality towards her own children that is the greatest taboo" (65). Those things deemed most taboo in our culture are usually those that hold the most truth. The undeniably physically and psychologically close bond between mother and child is that which fueled Kristeva's writing of "Stabat Mater." It is the image presented in the pieta. When it is missing, the identity formation of the child is at risk. For some, that means a floundering lack of identity. For others, such as Elphaba, it means some initial searching that leads to a victorious self-formation that culminates spectacularly on stage in "Defying Gravity." She sings, "I'm through with playing by the rules of someone else's game... I'm through accepting limits, cause someone says there so." She is almost ready to abandon the Symbolic order and enter her own jouissance, but hesitates, wanting Glinda to come with her. In the original staging, both women grasp Elphaba's broom, singing in perfect harmony, and the audience thinks,

2 THE MISSING MOTHER   27

for a moment, that Glinda might join Elphaba's cause, but she cannot leave the Symbolic. Ultimately, Elphaba must defy gravity on her own, singing, "And if I'm flying solo? At least I'm flying free!" (Schwartz) Flying free, defying gravity is Elphaba's jouissance. She can only do it alone and society, Oz, is frightened by its power. If Elphaba has been bound by the mother/daughter relationship, she would never have been able to make what is a fairly easy choice for her. She feels no obligation to others or to an other. She is free.

Freedom is also an important theme in *Billy Elliot*, as Billy gains autonomy from traditional gender stereotypes and the burden of being raised without his mom. Although not the focus of this study, it is worth mentioning the beauty and innovation of the number "Expressing Yourself" and the joy that song expresses. Michael, with the same caution to wind attitude about revolution that Marius expresses for a vastly different cause in *Les Miserable*, rebels against societal norms, dresses up in women's clothes, revels in the experience, and gives Billy the chance to try the same thing. While that means of gender experimentation does not interest Billy, breaking down gender stereotypes in other areas does, and so Michael, in this number, along with normalizing the experiences of countless young people, gives Billy the freedom to pursue his own rebellion through dance.

Ballet is Billy's act of rebellion against the social and genders norms of his hometown, deeply mired in the tradition and now plagued by a workers strike. In a first unwitting act of rebellion, Billy stays for the ballet class that follows his boxing lesson. While not passionate about pugilism, Billy loves ballet and excels at it. He, at first, hides his dance lesson from his father and friends, but is supported in his efforts by his ironically absent mother. His mother, who died several years prior to the opening of the story, is present both in Billy's memory and on stage, as a spectral character, with whom Billy frequently talks. In the heartbreaking song, "Dear Billy (Mum's Letter)," his mother, or Billy's imaginary projection of her, reads from the letter she wrote before she died;

> I will always be proud to have known you.
> Proud that you were mine
> Proud in everything
> And you must promise me this Billy
> In everything you do
> Always be yourself Billy. (Hall, 2006)

While Billy's mother is not actually present in this daily life, he has internalized her image. In psychoanalytic terms, this can be conceptualized several ways. Billy's internalization can be understood as the ultimate ending to the "Fort/Da Game" he observed with his own children. In the game, the child throws a toy away, "fort," and then regains possession of the object, "Da," thus allowing the child to develop a sense of object permanence or a feeling of control over the loss temporarily experienced when the child's parent is no longer in the room. While Billy has no control over his mother being taken away through death, in his mind, through his projection of her, he is able to control his feelings of loss and grief. In turning her absence into presence, he establishes a sense of identity and control that, while linked to her is not determined by her. In this way, her absence is an ironically positive experience.

Billy's projections of and conversations with his dead mother can also be interpreted through the lens of the transitional object. First introduced as a theory in 1951, in *Playing and Reality*, D. W. Winnicott writes, "I have introduced the terms 'transitional objects' and 'transitional phenomena' for designation of the intermediate area of experience, between the thumb and the teddy bear, between the oral erotism and the true object-relationship, between creative activity and projection of what has already been introjected, between primary unawareness of indebtedness and the acknowledgement of indebtedness" (2). More simply put, the transitional object is that which an infant will use as an intermediary between his relationship with the mother established primarily through breast-feeding and thus reduced to the breast by some scholars, and his relationship with the world. It is the thing that allows the infant to establish control and a unique sense of self. Winnicott is explicit in his writing that the transitional object, unlike Klien's internal object, is a physical thing. It is the blankie, stuffed animal or toy, commonly that the infant cannot "live" without. In "The Location of Cultural Experience," Winnicott writes, "... loss of object means to the child a loss of the play area, and loss of meaningful symbol. In favorable circumstances the potential space becomes filled with the products of the baby's own creative imagination" (Rudnytsky ed., 1993). In *Billy Elliot*, Billy lost his play space when his mother died. The boxing ring is the immediate substitute, but that space does not allow for creative exploration. Instead, the space of the dance floor and of dance itself becomes the potential space and Billy's projections of his mother are as much developments of his creative imagination, both before and after he begins dancing, as dancing itself. Here, his mother's physical absence gives rise to his transitional object and to the place of creative expression that eventually allows Billy enough autonomy not to need his spectral mother any longer. The Reprise of "Dear Billy" ends with Billy's "Bye Mum." He is ready for her absence to be permanent. He dismisses her, with no angry, or grief, simply stating that he is comfortable enough to be without her. Her absence has allowed him to grow and develop his own sense of self. He is autonomous now.

For Billy, his mother's absence has a positive result, but that is not always true. The relationships between mothers and children in *Spring Awakening* vary widely with different implications, but the absence of mothers or their silence is certainly a theme pervades the musical. *Spring Awakening* was originally written my Frank Wedekind and published in 1891 in Germany. At that time, the play was considered scandalous because of its unabashed examinations of teenage sexuality, rape, sexual abuse, and abortion, not to mention the criticism levied against parenting norms and the German educational system. The 2006 musical written by Sater and Sheik only sanitizes one aspect of the original script—the sex between Mechior and Wendla is consensual. Of the musical's three protagonists, two have mothers who are noticeably absent or silent.

Moritz Stiefel is the brooding, anxiety-ridden best friend of Melchior Gabor, who at the play's beginning, seems to be perfect. He is smart, handsome, and popular with both teachers and students. Moritz is laughed at by his teachers, classmates, and the young women of the town, who know that his future is insecure, at best, because he lacks intellectual prowess. Puberty frightens him, as he does not understand his physical responses or the desires which prompt those responses. He speaks often of his fear of his father, who is established as authoritarian and unyielding. When Moritz finds out that he has not passed his exams and will not advance to the next grade, thus ending his academic career, his father is brutal, belittling him and any future he might have. His mother is noticeably missing from the conversation. In fact, Moritz's biological mother is missing throughout; without her, he has little buffer or defense against his father and instead turns to Melchior's mother, Mrs. Gabor, to fill that role.

Melchior's mother is established as the ideal parent from Wedekind's perspective. Unlike Moritz's or Melchior's father or Wendla's mother, Mrs. Gabor is honest with both Melchior and Moritz. She does not impose her will or her morality upon the boys; she does not chastise their curiosity or stifle their desire to learn about their bodies and their world. When she comes upon them reading *Faust*, she mentions that the sexual component might be difficult for them to understand, but she does not censor their reading. She realizes they need to learn. She realizes that boys need autonomy and trusts both them and herself enough to grant that. Moritz, however, is not yet ready for such freedom. Instead, and perhaps because he lacked a relationship of significance with his own mother, he needs Mrs. Gabor to coddle him.

After he is expelled he writes to Mrs. Gabor, begging her for the money needed to sail to American. In "And Then There Were None," her response is interspersed with Moritz's defense. Her letter to him is a study in pseudo-mother relationship. It begins, "Dear Her Stiefel, / Moritz, /I've spent the entire day thinking about your note. / Truly it touched me, it did, that you'd think of me as a friend" (Sater, 2006). There are both notes of intimacy and distance juxtaposed against each other. The idea of an older woman, thinking about the "note" of a young man definitely, has sexual overtones, especially immediately followed by the words "truly it touched me" with the repeated "it did." That "it did" though, given for emphasis, highlights and contradicts the initial sexual implications, as it seems to be a mechanism to reinforce a feeling that is only superficially present. Her tone remains detached as she informs him, "I cannot provide the money your request" for his passage to America, ostensibly to escape the repression and shame he now feels, and uses the odd negative phrasing, "You would do me wrong, Her Stiefel to read into my refusal any lack of affection" (Sater, 2006). In his perspective, and from her own words, she cares, but not enough, she understands, but will not intervene. Her character is static, a good mother, who does not interfere, but allows children to make choices and even mistakes, something unheard of in today's world of helicopter and snowplow parenting. Ironically though, this is not the mother that Moritz needs. Because of the absence of his own mother, and because of the stifling atmosphere in which he has been raised, he expects to be smothered, either by distain or love. Since he has faced distain, he seeks the opposite, but Frau Gabor cannot give that. She is willing to defend him and his actions, to help him take responsibility, to help him grow, again, as a "good" mother should, but that is not what he wants. He wants to be coddled and saved. When his substitute mother cannot do that, Moritz takes the worst possible action, ending his life by suicide.

Wendla, whose mother in *Spring Awakening* is also partially absent, also dies before the musical's end. Her death, however, is even more directly related to her mother's absence than is Moritz's. Frau Bergman is not physically absence. The audience meets her in the play's first scene, in which the audience also sees how she is missing. Wendla's older sister, married and living in her own home, has just given birth to her second child and Wendla, a young teenager, wants to understand pregnancy and childbirth. The play opens with Wendla, center stage, in her white shift dress, now too short for her, singing, "Mama who bore me / Mama who gave me / No way to handle things/ Who made me so sad / Mama the weeping / Mama the angels / No sleep in heaven, or Bethlehem" (Sater, 2006). This short verse is fraught with the difficulties of the mother/child dyad. Frau Bergman has given her daughter life, but nothing that she needs to live. Wendla intuits the connections between death (heaven) and Bethlehem (birth), but she is missing the links that her mother refuses to provide. In the dialogue that follows, Wendla begs her mother to explain intercourse and childbirth, offering to hide under her mother's skirts, in an ironic depiction of pregnancy, so her mother can talk freely without having to face her daughter and still she refuses, holding fast to the story of the stork, which Wendla knows is absurd. Her mother, locked the image of mother as virgin, not able to accept the sexuality that accompanies traditional motherhood, or her own daughter's budding sexuality, she attempts to foreclose on all possibility of her daughter having a sexual relationship, but that, of course, fails. Wendla enters into a sexual relationship, with as much consent as she can give, not actually knowing what intercourse is or its ramifications, with Melchior. That encounter ends in her pregnancy, which again, her mother hides from her, telling her she is instead, anemic. Wendla goes on to die from the complications of a botched abortion, to which she has not given consent. The stunning lack of knowledge the Wendla begs for from her mother, which ultimately destroys her, is a form of absence. While physically overbearing, the mother's lack of communication functions as a form of absence. Jacqueline Rose aptly describes this when she writes, "Mothers, of course, are classically thought of as containers, the Greek idea of the womb as a purely passive receptacle being perhaps the most egregious version of them all. But, that a mother contains is surely true; inside her body and then again when she hold her baby. In one psychoanalytic model, it then also falls to her to contain or mange on its own behalf – which is why a mother who pushes away difficult feelings, too eager to turn away from pain and rage, to decency and cheer is useless" (124). Rose's meditate here is completely accurate of Mrs. Bergman. She wants to hide and sanitize bit of life that she fears Wendla cannot handle. She tries to suppress Wendla's growth into womanhood and desire for knowledge, but while the classical imagery presents women as containers, women cannot be contained. Wendla, in the absence of her mother's guidance, seeks knowledge on her own, and it destroys her.

In a scene that rings true to Wedekind's original Naturalistic and Expressionistic overtones, Wendla sings "Whispering" which recounts Moritz's funeral and her pregnancy, while foreshadowing her own death. She sings, "Listening ... / To the souls in the fools night / Fumbling mutely with their rude hands / And there's heartache without end" (Sater, 2006). She and Melchior were the fumbling souls who have caused enormous heartache, most significantly to themselves. Wendla knows she is a disappointment in her mother's eyes, singing, "History ... / Little miss didn't do right / Went and ruined all the true plans / Such a shame, such a sin" (Sater, 2006). The final two lines of that verse are not in Wendla's perspective, but in her mother's. It is the mother's chastisement that she rehearses, but does not believe. Wendla has never embraced her mother's lack. She has fought against it, with this song her final stand: "And he touched me and I let him love me / So let that be my story." While in the phrasing, Wendla doesn't give herself agency over the act, she acknowledges her will and consent. The strength of "So let that be my story," (Sater, 2006) with the multiple strong consonants giving the line vocal power and determination also allows Wendla the agency that her mother's absence has taken from her. Her mother's effectual and emotional absence has left her with the ability to formulate her own desire, but Mrs. Bergman's physical presence means that Wendla is still oppressed. As Morel writes, "The signifier of the desire of the mother, *signifier of an absence* which would become a lack, need to be distinguished from these maternal words which have the force of law, and which rather testify to an *excess of presence*, as in the case of the mother who commits infanticide." In all ways meaningful, Mrs. Bergman is absent, which should give her daughter the ability to self create, but in the practical sense, she is there stifling her, governing her, and ultimately killing her.

There are two girls in *Spring Awakening*, whose mothers are functionally absent, but who survive. Martha and Ilsa sing "The Dark I Know Well" about the abuse, both physical and sexual, that they endure at the hands of their fathers and other men, while their mothers ignore the horrors their daughters face. Martha describes to her friends the physical abuse she faces every night at home when they discover the welts on her legs while walking home from school. Martha describes daily beatings, explaining that it is because her parents, particularly her father, love her so much they beat her to show their concern. In dialogue, interestingly, she does not mention the sexual abuse, but in lyric, she sings, "You say, 'Time for bed now child.' / Mom just smiles that smile. Just like she never saw me. / Just like she never saw me" (Sater, 2006). The repetition of the last sentence is most important, as it emphasizes the absence. Martha's mother pretends that nothing is wrong, that her daughter's pain does not exist, while, from Martha's perspective, the pain begins with her mother's purposeful ignorance. Martha needs her mother to be her advocate, but her mother is unable to. To be Martha's advocate, her mother would need to be fully connected to her daughter. She would need to be in position of the absolute abject, ready to receive the abject material that her daughter is forced to receive: the blood from the beatings, the semen from the sexual encounters. Her mother, who has already divorced herself from that material, is unwilling to take it back. Martha must struggle though on her own. She survives and is at least still alive at the end of the show, as is Ilsa.

The audience learns, through her conversation with Moritz just before his suicide, that Ilsa's mother has effectively abandoned her by not allowing her to return home. Ilsa has turned to life as an artist's model, a prostitute really, the audience assumes, in part because of the abuse she faced at home, but is trying to go home, as that environment is a known evil, instead of the partially unknown evil she faces on the streets. She longs to return to childhood and encourages Melchior to join her in an attempt to regain the innocence they both have lost, but he refuses. Without her former playmate, she cannot pursue the games of childhood she remembers, but she continues back to her house, in an attempt to save herself. Her mother has been absent for too long and her attempt to return to childhood play is not really an attempt at return but at revision. She is seeking a way to reclaim her childhood on her terms, to erase the abuse she faced and still faces, because her mother, like Martha's refused to intervene or defend. Ilsa finally does reclaim power through nature, in the absence of her mother, who is never present on stage, when she sings the musical's closing song, "Purple Summer."

"Purple Summer" describes the beauty of late summer sunset with nature, robust, and alive buzzing around, and it is Ilsa who gives the generative images of flourishing crops and newborn foals voice, as she sings, "I will sing the song of purple summer" (Sater, 2006). She has overcome her mother's absence, despite the way in which it threatened to destroy her.

Perhaps the character most able to overcome her mother's functional absence is Natalie in 2008s *Next to Normal*. This brilliant musical is an honest, sometimes brutal, sometimes funny exploration of family dynamics in the wake of bipolar disorder. Diana, the mother, played originally by Alice Ripley, has suffered from increasingly difficult to control mental illness since the death of her infant son nearly eighteen years prior to the time in which the musical is set. Her daughter, Natalie, is a budding piano virtuoso, who, despite her excellent grades and outstanding talent, perceives herself as invisible to her mother, who longs for and is intensely preoccupied with her dead son. Natalie is aware of her mother's inability to connect with her, singing, "Superboy and the Invisible Girl / Son of Steel and Daughter of Air / He's a hero, a lover, a prince / She's not there" (Yorkey, 2009). Natalie knows her brother has been elevated to mythic status, and she is less than human, in her mother's eyes. She is nothing, not even his lyrical antithesis, she is less than that, but she wishes that she was. She reiterates, "He's not here / I am here" (Yorkey, 2009). The insistence of the word "here" in the lyric indicates an attempt to make her position in her mother's life more permanent that she knows it is.

Several scenes later, Diana confirms what her daughter has already articulated in "Superboy and Invisible Girl," that Diana purposefully refuses connection with her daughter. During hypnotherapy with Dr. Madden, Diana remembers, "We had Natalie to ... And I know she knows. I could hold her in the hospital. I couldn't let myself hold her" (Yorkey, 2009). To preserve the pure, untarnished and completely fantasized relationship she has with her dead son, Diana cannot allow herself to bond with her living daughter. In "Stabat Mater," Kristeva's essay divides into two parallel sections: the first, an academic argument on the relationship between feminism and motherhood; the second stream of consciousness assessment of her own experience as a new mother. She writes:

My body is no longer mine, it writes, suffers, bleeds, catches cold, bites, slavers, coughs, breaks out in a rash, and laughs. Yet when his, my son's joy returns, his smile cleanses only my eyes. But suffering, his suffering – that I feel inside; that never remains separate or alien but embraces me at once without a moment's respite. As if I had brought not a child but suffering into the world and it, suffering, refused to leave me, insisted on coming back, on haunting me, permanently. One does not beat children in pain, it's pain that one bears; the child is pain's representative and once delivered moves in for good. Obviously, you can close your eyes, stop up your ears, teach courses, run errands, clean house, think about things, about ideas. But a mother is also marked by pain, succumbs to it. (138)

This passage reads as if Yorkey and Kit used it to inform every aspect of Diana's character and relationship with her son. Gabe is quite literally a part of Diana; when he died, she subsumed him into her and he is her life, in a contemporary obverse of myth of Zeus and Athena. Diana longs for an insular bubble in which she could protect Gabe, and by extension herself, from the outside world, from illness of both body and mind. The only experience she can process or wants to process is the enormity of her suffering, which she has taken back from her dying infant, but in the process she has locked out her daughter, who knows she is her mother's consolation prize. Even has Diana may have wanted to overcome her grief, she stands in her own way, not allowing herself to bond with her daughter. She is unwilling to allow herself the maternal space to love one child along with or in place of another. She is also unwilling to give up the mirage of her dead son, causing her to be both functionally absent and overwhelmingly present in her daughter's life. Because Natalie, who is sixteen, lives with her parents, her mother is physically and excruciatingly present in her daily life. In the musical's opening song, Diana finds Natalie awake at four o'clock on the morning and tries to express concern for her daughter's well-being, but also tell her daughter, "I'm going to have sex with your father, now" (Yorkey, 2009) which naturally disgusts Natalie. In all ways related to daily life, Diana is present, almost too present, but in terms of emotional care and support, Diana is functionally absent.

The assumption is that her daughter forced to grow up without a "normal" mother would become a delinquent with no direction or moral compass. That opposite is true. Natalie is straight A student and near prodigy on the piano. She is practicing consistently through the show, for her recital and her Julliard audition. She is focused and determined to use her intellect and talent to escape from her mother. As her relationship with Henry, a boy from school develops, she allows herself, begrudgingly to live as a "normal" teenager, even to experiment with marijuana, but she remains, at the end of the play, the focused mature adult woman of the Goodman family. Her mother's absence has created a forced self-reliance and she has assumed that as her identity. The complication is that Natalie's identity is a compromise formation, and while upon first glance an audience can be proud of how self-sufficient and self-directed. she is those qualities are reaction formations, and may or may not be Natalie's true self. Her mother's absence has forced her to become something. If her mother was there to guide her, perhaps her personality would have been very different. Ironically, her mother's absence has forced Natalie into being a Type A stereotype instead of leaving her the freedom to develop her own character.

At the end of *Next to Normal*, Diana's functional absence becomes physical absence. She is no longer able to navigate the two worlds in which she is living: the façade of her family life and the throws of her psychosis. She considers ending her fight and giving into her hallucinations completely in the "Make Up Your Mind / Catch Me I'm Falling (Reprise)" when she sings, "Catch me I'm falling / Sinking and sprawling / Maybe I'll let myself fall" (Yorkey, 2009). Dan, her husband, begs her to "stay with me / try again" but she has lost her will to continue in that "Maybe I've lost it at last / Maybe my last lucid moment has past / I'm dancing with death, I suppose / But really, who knows?" (Yorkey, 2009). Dan is unable to see the reality of his wife's situation. He wants her to stay, to try to function in society. He longs for the "normal" life of Lacan's Symbolic register. That is the position in which the subject is locked into the paternal, law-giving, conventional order of the world. It is what most people exist in every day. Diana is beyond that. She teeters on the end of the Real every day and touches her jouissance every time she "sees" Gabe, her dead son who lives in her hallucinations. She is completely unwilling to let that go. It truly brings her joy, despite the pain her unwillingness or inability to grieve and move on causes the rest of her family.

By the end of the musical though, Diana has enough clarity to recognize and articulate her psychosis. She cannot control it, of course, but she can make choices about it and she chooses to leave, to stay with her parents. The audience could be tempted to read that as Diana's attempt to return to her own childhood, but without any other clues to such a desire earlier in the musical, it is more likely that her parents' home simply offers a safe space for her, that does not require practical planning and life skills which she does not possess.

After Diana explains her decision to Dan, she also sings to Natalie in "Make Up Your Mind / Catch Me I'm Falling (Reprise)," "And maybe you feel that way too / I see me in you / A girl full of anger and hope / A girl with a mother who just couldn't cope / A girl who felt caught, and felt no one could see / But maybe one day she'll be free" (Yorkey, 2009). Diana recognizes the pain she has caused to her daughter and has a wish that Natalie be able to overcome it. It is, however, nearly too late for Natalie to care.

She responds, "It's so lovely that you're sharing / No really, I'm all ears / But where has all this caring been for sixteen years / For all those years I'd prayed that you'd go away for good / Half the time afraid that you really would / When I thought you might be dying /I cried for all we'd never be / But, they'll be no more crying / Not for me (5x)" (Yorkey, 2009). Natalie has all the pointed sarcasm of a typical teenage girl, combined with the enormity of responsibility and pain with which she has lived since birth. Like her mother, she faces an internal struggle of wanting to be free of her mother, and simultaneously terrified of that near-reality. When Natalie tells her mother of all the tears she has shed, she is describing the abjection that she has undergone. Typically, according to Kristeva, it is the mother's body which abjects itself and is subject to abjection via all mothering processes, especially birth and breast-feeding, but here, Diana's inability to mother Natalie has forced her into the position of self-mothering. She is abjected one, crying. At the end of the musical though, she has completed the process of abjection; she is no longer crying. She is ready to let go.

Diana is too; "Maybe we can't be ok / But maybe we're tough and we'll try anyway / We'll live with what's real / Let go of what's past / And, maybe I'll see you at last" (Yorkey, 2009). Diana is choosing her real, with her dead son instead of her living daughter, but in that choice, she is hopeful that she will be able to recognize both of her children for who or what they really are. Any illusion of a perfect life or family has been shattered for Natalie and she is mature enough to know that such illusions only life in a Symbolic façade. In that respect, she is like her mother. She does not want the pretense of perfection. She explains, "I don't need a life that's normal / That's way too far away / But something next to normal would be ok. / Yes, something next to normal / that's the thing I'd like to try / Close enough to normal to get by" (Yorkey, 2009). Natalie wants the space, returned from the Real, that is a compromise formation, allowing a person who understands psychosis to be able to live in society.

Still she worries, saying to Henry "I might end up crazy" (Yorkey, 2009) in "Hey #3/Perfect for You," but he assures her that doesn't matter to him. He is younger and still far more innocent than she is. Natalie recognizes the cycle of which she is a part. Natalie understands that she is at risk, if she aims too high, but she is, at least, free as is Diana. Diana is the only absent mother, discussed here, whose outcome the audience knows. Following Diana is a remarkably progressive move for a commercial Broadway musical, whose normal aim is to maintain the societal status quo and a mother who leaves her child is definitely not plot that audiences like to acknowledge.

The figure of the absent or functionally absent mother is remarkable the vastly different ways the absence can effect her and her children. For some, such as Moritz and Wendla, the functionally absent mother, damns her child to death. For others, like Elphaba and Natalie, the absent mother gives freedom. Regardless of the outcome for the child, in each of these musicals, the ending gives the audience what is expected. The audience pities the child, either as audience cathartically grieves for the child, or as the audience roots for the child who now is forced to go on without maternal guidance.

CHAPTER 3

The Overbearing Mother

Abstract This chapter explores the figure of the overbearing mother, with *Gypsy* as the example par excellence. It is a necessary exploration into the ways in which common stereotypes intersect with feminist literary theory. We see this in the fantasized mother/son relationship in *Next to Normal* as a mechanism for coping with her perception of her failure as a mother. *Matilda* and *The 25th Annual Putnam County Spelling Bee* are comedic examples of the overbearing mother figure, whose children give voice to their detrimental presence. *Spring Awakening* also offers this figure to audiences in the form of Wendla's mother, whose strict conservativism leads to her daughter's demise in the guise of maternal protection.

Keywords Overbearing · Narcissism · Inferiority · Mirror stage

The overbearing mother is the parental figure with whom most Broadway afficianados are familiar, due almost exclusively to the domination of the character of Mama Rose in the collective Broadway imagination. Mama Rose, the stage mother extraordinaire in *Gypsy*, has become synonymous with any mother, particularly in entertainment fields, who longs to live vicariously through the success of potential success of her child. In the case of *Gypsy*, Mama Rose first looks to June to be her substitute self/star and when June unexpectedly runs away, to Louise,

© The Author(s) 2019
G. M. MacKenzie, *Maternal Representations in Twenty-First Century Broadway Musicals*, Pivotal Studies in the Global American Literary Imagination, https://doi.org/10.1007/978-3-030-32337-0_3

her much more reticent younger daughter. When even casual theatre-goers think of mothers on the musical stage, they are likely to picture Mama Rose, played by any of the greats: Ethel Merman, Tyne Daly, Bernadette Peters, or Patti LuPone. She is ubiquitous. Perhaps that is because until the middle of the twenty-first century, she was the only mother on the musical stage who was written with any level of psychological depth and vocal role to match. Dating back to 1959, *Gypsy*, whose lyrics in part belong to the tongue-twisting genius Stephen Sondheim, then just getting started in his Broadway career and haunted by mother issues himself, the musical is remarkably forward thinking. After *Gypsy*, it took Broadway another fifty years to match that level of exploration of the role of the mother.

Overbearing mothers, such as Mama Rose, are the product of complex psychological forces. To understand the figure itself, one must return to the ideas of Kristeva and Cixous. Kristeva's work on la langue is particularly important in understanding this theatrical figure. According to Kristeva's work, the mother uses the child as her access point to the Other. The Other is the externalization of the internal locus of social and sexual relations. As Kristeva explains, "[I]t is precisely the child that, for a *mother* (as opposed to a *genetrix*), constitutes an *access* (an excess) toward the Other. The child is the removal of what was only a graft during pregnancy; an *alter ego* capable (or not) or replacing a maternal narcissism henceforce intergrated with a 'being for it'" (*Desire in Language*, 279). The child is for the mother, the literal and physical manifestation of the mother's desire for the Other. The child acts as the conduit. When the child is born and the infant grows to no longer depend on the mother, the mother's access to her own desire is foreclosed. To stave off that elimination, the overbearing mother creates ties that infanticize the child and create dependency and rivalry.

Rivalry is a concept not often overtly articulated, but that can be traced through the history of psychoanalytic theory. Joan Riviere in *Love, Hate and Reparation* articulates the concept best and most concisely. She writes, "The impulse towards competitiveness, and rivalry in general, is drawn from many interacting sources, self-preservative, sexual and aggressive" (36). The rivalry of the mother/child, particularly mother/daughter dyad inacts each of these tenants. The mother attempts to overtake her child, as an act of self-preservation. The child is a narcissistic projection outward, but when that projection begins to differentiate herself or break away, the mother seeks to subsume the child so that she is not fractured, but is able to maintain the illusion of wholeness and completion. As the mother attempts to reabsorb the child, she is able to return to a state of pre-maternity, a state when she is a sexual being. Rivalry in the mother/child dyad mimics that of the rivalry of the state of womanhood itself in which a woman is either mother or whore. She is either a sexual being or a mother. The obvious fact that most cases of motherhood stem from a sexual act is glossed over by society. To remedy the perceived sexual split, the mother competes with her child to attain greater sexual prowess through acts that enhance her conventional attractiveness or by projecting her sexuality onto her child so as to make the child and then herself by association, by more desirable, or by the observe acts to diminish the child's attractiveness. Riviere's description of the attraction to inferiority explains this, in part:

> [I]n a milder form this is an exceedingly common character-trait; many people are really happy and contented only with those in some way inferior to themselves – it may be intellectually, or by class standards, or even morally inferior. These inferior ones are the people they really need are dependent on in life. Those who need inferiors to consort with are of course the converse of snobs, but both they and the snobs seek the same thing at the heart in different ways. Both need reassurance and a guarantee that they are not poor, mean and empty, unworthy and unlovable in themselves. (37)

When the mother is overbearing, she deflates the worth of the child, so as to support her own worth. As the inferior child is now in the supporting role, the mother can be the star, or in psychoanalytic terms, the child is still ironically in the position of power, as it is she who is acting as Other, defining the mother's desire, even as the mother believes she is the one in control. The difference between actual and perceived desire is another form of the sexual rivalry Riviere describes.

Rivalry, for Riviere, can also give rise to aggression. Melanie Klein, in contrast, explains that for many, motherhood is " … long-postponed fulfillment of an all-important wish [that] tends to make her [the mother] less aggressive and to increase her capacity for loving her child" (77). However, diminished aggression happens only in ideal situations. As Klein goes on to explain, "[S]ome mothers, as we know, exploit this relationship for the gratification of their own desires, i.e. their possessiveness and the satisfaction of having somebody dependent upon them. Such women want their children to cling to them, and they hate them to grow up and to acquire individualities of their own" (77–78). The aggressive jealousy described here is a near perfect summation of the overbearing mother, whose need to outshine her child frequently takes the form of aggressive smothering.

Such is the case of the quintessential stage mother, Mama Rose in *Gypsy*. *Gypsy* is truly a remarkable musical. It debuted on Broadway in 1959 with book by Arthur Laurents, music by Jules Styne, and lyrics by Stephen Sondheim, whose own mother issues are well documented by his biographer, Meryl Secrest. The power of this musical, which critics including Jack Viertel and Raymond Knapp consider one of the best ever staged, has been revived on Broadway four times, most recently in both 2003 and 2008, which testifies to its enormous resonance. It is interesting to note that *Gypsy*, despite critical praise and enduring power over an audience and box office, did not win the Tony Award for Best Musical and have never won the Tony for Best Revival of a Musical. Perhaps, that is because, as Ethan Mordden writes, "[I]t says that your mother doesn't love you. She loves what she thinks you can do for her" (48). That brutal honesty is clear in the telling. The musical is the story of Mama Rose and her efforts to make her daughters, first June and then Louise, famous on the already dying vaudeville circuit. She is simultaneously brash and woefully naïve. This is the position in which we find Mama Rose near the beginning of the show. In *The Secret Life of the American Musical*, Jack Viertel writes about Mama Rose, "She's the most powerful person onstage as *Gypsy* begins, and its made blindingly clear that the least powerful is not Uncle Jocko, whom she berates, but poor pathetic Louise, so paralyzed by fear that she can barely move to hide behind her sister. The trajectory of *Gypsy* is such that by the evening's end, the two characters will have exactly switched places. Louise will be in charge of everything, and her mother will be reduced to wearing a borrowed fur over her frumpy dress while begging to come to a showbiz party in Louise's honor" (36). The fate of the overbearing mother here is the radical rebellion of the long subdued daughter. That trajectory can be traced through the show's musical numbers.

The "I Want" or "Ask" song is a convention of musical theatre that happens near the beginning of Act 1. It identifies the protagonist's main goal and frequently gives a timeline or road map for how the protagonist intends to proceed. "Some People" is that song for Rose, in which she sings, "I had a dream, / A wonderful dream, Poppa, / All about June and the Orpheum Circuit – / Gimmie a chance and I know I can / Work it" (Sondheim, 1959). Her want is for her daughter, but only as it will bring her fame and glory. As Viertel analyzes the lyric, "[T]here's nothing generic about Rose. Her specific description of vaudeville defines her and teaches us some things we might not know" (58). The audience learns of her particular view of vaudeville and performance through her specific images, such as "velvet curtains" for the backdrop and "a feathered hat for the baby." Her idea of show business is all flash and spectacle. It is about "the number" reducing the performers to set pieces, privileging the show itself over the players. Rose is the absolute bastardization of the Aristotelean idea of drama. In *Poetics*, Aristotle outlines and prioritizes the six elements of a good drama: plot, character, thought, diction, music, and spectacle. For Aristotle, the unification of the plot is the most important element, with spectacle, or what contemporary audiences recognize as set, costume, lighting, and sound design. Spectacle is Rose's only interest. There is no substance to the act she is creating. The void in June's number reflects the disconnection between Rose and June. Rose cannot see the rift growing between them because she is only interested in superficial success. She doesn't take time to know her daughter's deeper desires. Rose has no awareness of June's desires or her true character. Ironically, in her quest to create the perfect number, ostensibly for her younger daughter, June, what she does is enhance her own character. Each time she tries to improve "the number," she increases her own presence both on stage and in the lives of her children until "the number" is co-opted by her older daughter, Louise.

In Raymond Knapp's *The American Musical and the Performance of Personal Identity*, he explores the ways in which musical characters shape their own identities on stage. In Gypsy, the shaping of one character's identity comes at the cost of another; "[A]t the start of the musical, mother and daughter are poles apart, with Louise desperately needing the approval of Mme. Rose, who seems scarcely aware of her older daughter's existence except to criticize her inadequate performance in support of her younger sister, June, the show's star. But at the end, after everyone else leaves them the two characters merge. According to Laurents, the intent was 'that Gypsy *becomes* Rose'" (217). If Gypsy becomes Rose, if the daughter becomes the mother, then the overbearing mother figure has been deflated by the sharp edge of the once dull daughter figure. This is the culmination of the rivalry Riviere describes.

Interestingly, in a Lacanian sense, Knapp draws out the parallels between naming and power for both women. He points out,

> [T]hat the two share a name – Louise's birth name is Rose Lousie – odes not emerge until fairly late in the second act, after which Louise herself is rapidly eclipsed in favor of the stripper personality she will become, a process tracked deftly by the changes made to her name. First she merges somewhat clumsily with her mother, as 'Louise' becomes 'Rose Louise' and displaces her mother in the title of the new act, 'Rose Louise and her Hollywood Blondes' (a makeover of the failing 'Madame Rose's Toreadorables'). Then, when Rouse Louise is preparing to debut as a stripper, she becomes, '*Gypsy* Rose Louise,' adding the name that describes them both, since 'Gypsy' may designate – when it does not refer to a specific ethnic group – either dancers (on Broadway) or all those who, like Rose Louise and her mother, travel the country as independents taking whatever jobs they can get. Finally, 'Louise' disappears altogether when the announcer misread the card, a seemingly random event that carries great significance because it marks the moment when the now-familiar name, 'Gypsy Rose Lee' take its final form. (217–218)

Naming is an act of power. It is one of the first acts of domination a parent has over the child. When a mother names her child, she is marking that child with her will. When the mother uses her own name in the child's name, she is engaging in an overt act of narcissistic projection. Mama Rose, naming her older daughter Rose Louise after herself, is an act of hope in the potential of that child to live out her dreams vicariously. When the show opens, and it is already evident to Rose that her older daughter is not the child who will make her dreams come true, she drops Rose from her name, choosing to call her and have the audience recognize her only as Louise. A shared name was favorable when the child has potential but Rose wanted to eschew that closeness when the potential was diminished.

Ironically, as Louise begins to assert herself and her own identity more, she, in part, takes back her mother's name, implying that she recognizes their similarities and wants to showcase them. It is also Louise's attempt to gain a closeness with her mother that she has never had, through the connection of the name which symbolizes the dream of stardom coming to fruition. Of course by the end, Gypsy's stardom is the opposite of her mother's vision, but is her own vision of self, laid bare before the audience.

Each example of overbearing motherhood can have a different effect on the child. For younger daughter June, Rose's overbearing nature has a nearly stereotypical outcome. The more her mother asserts her will, the more June resists until she leaves. Partially because of the societal expectations of the time during which the play was set and written, and partially to produce a greater contrast to Louise's own assertion of will at the end of the play, June does not run away alone. She elopes with Tulsa, a boy from the act on who Louise has also had a crush. June's final act of defiance does not help to change Rose's behavior. Instead, she switches her attention to June. In "Everything's Coming Up Roses," Rose desperately asserts that she will create a star. It takes her only one slightly hesitant line in the first verse: "[T]hey think that we're through, but baby, ..." (Sondheim, 1959). For just a second, Rose admits that to the rest of the vaudeville community, her entire world, she has no chance of success, but she immediately recovers, at least in lyric. As she sings, she interestingly switches her emphasis between her daughter and her role in her daughter's success;

> Now's your inning. Stand the world on its ear?
> Set it spinning! That'll be just the beginning?
> Curtain up! Light the lights!
> You got nothing to do but the heights!
> You'll be swell. You'll be great.
> I can tell. Just you wait.
> That lucky star I talk about is due!
> Honey, everything's coming up roses for me and for you!
> (Sondheim, 1959)

As the song retards at the end, the emphasis on each word increases until those five words, " ... for me and for you!" are drilled into the audience's consciousness just before the curtain falls for Act 1. Belted out, like a demand on the universe, Rose insists that Louise now be subject to greater pressure and scrutiny for her mother's dreams to come true. The effect is the opposite of what Rose could imagine at this point. Louise internalizes her mother demand, and abject material. If we remember what Kristeva explains, the abject is the refuse spilled out of bodies of both mother and child that the mother must manage. Here, Louise has no chance to go through the process of abjection. Instead, she must take all the refuse her mother dumps upon her. What she does with it, though, is remarkable. Instead of letting her mother's overbearing nature, the result of abjection gone wrong, destroy her, she slowly refines it in her own raw power. Louise doesn't work to refine the abject; she revels in it, taking the advice of the other burlesque performers she meets, to find a "gimmick." Her gimmick, a bold direct address of the audience, is a modification of the brashness her mother has displayed throughout the entire show. Louise takes her mother's overbearing insistence and turns it into a desirous but insistent plea, "Let Me Entertain You," taking a song from an early version of their vaudeville act and making it her own. With subtle persistence and quiet resistance, Louise has overcome her mother's desires. For Louise, Rose's overbearing nature has a positive impact. She works within the perimeters her mother has established to find her own act. In turn, she also gains fame and sexual power and freedom. Such a positive outcome is rarely the case for those afflicted with overbearing mothers.

The opposite is true for Rapunzel in Sondheim's *Into the Woods*. First staged on Broadway in 1987 and revived in 2002 for Broadway and in 2012 for Shakespeare in the Park, *Into the Woods* is a mash-up of classic fairytales: Cinderella, Rapunzel, Jack and the Beanstalk, the Baker's Wife, and Little Red Riding Hood. Act 1 weaves the tales together and leads to their positive happy ever afters. Act 2 brings the audience to the aftermath of happily ever after, where characters have to face themselves and their ennui. While there are multiple mother/child relationships in the musical, it is the relationship between Rapunzel and her mother, the Witch, that is most filled with tension and sorrow. Their first onstage interaction, "Our Little World," is one of the least known songs from the musical, but it establishes their co-dependent relationship. The Witch is obviously overbearing, having locked Rapunzel in a tower from which she has no escape, but she is also, at least in part, content to be there, singing "Brushing my hair / Combing my hair / Only my mother/ And me and my hair / Our little world." Her hair, the third party in this completely insular relationship will become the mechanism for escape, but not yet. Here it is the hair, and the care surrounding it which stands for the entire relationship. It binds them together and, as the Witch points out, distracts Rapunzel, even as she begins to doubt her captivity, singings, "Our little world is perfect / Or at least so she claims." While the Witch too knows things are changing for her and her daughter "If what was growing / Was only her hair / And not her / That I'd prefer" (Sondheim, 1987), she does not impose any additional constraints on her daughter, believing the intensity of their bond is enough to keep Rapunzel in her place.

It is not, of course, and when the prince comes calling, she leaves, as her mother's attention has shifted to the Baker and his quest to deliver to her the four items that will allow her to resume her figure as a beautiful enchantress instead of an old hag, a curse placed on her by her own mother. The curse placed on the Witch by her own mother doubles the depiction of mother's as overbearing in this family's lineage. As the Witch explains to Rapunzel after she has escaped, "Ah, but I am old and ugly / I embarrass you / You are ashamed of me / You are ashamed / You don't understand" (Sondheim, 1987) it is, in part, because of her own hideous appearance and lack of confidence that the Witch has placed Rapunzel in the tower. She believes her daughter will not love her if she sees the beauty of the rest of the world. That is why it is so important that her wish only come true after her daughter has escaped. Once the Baker and his wife have gathered the required materials for the Witch's potion, she brews the elixir that will give them a child, but it also, she believe, will give her back her child, as it will return her to her beauty. Meryl Secrest reminds her readers, "[A]t that pivotal point, she sheds her cloak, her crone-like features, and her rags to emerge as a young woman in all her satin-clad glory. That is also the moment when she loses her magical powers" (356). The Witch deludes herself and the audience into seeing her overbearing nature as a result of her physical deformity, as if locking her daughter in a tower is just overcompensation for her own insecurity. That insecurity, the result of the loss of her physical attractiveness, is the result of her betrayal of her own mother.

Hence the audience is presented with a chain of overbearing mothers and the consequences of them. Rapunzel's grandmother, who the audience only knows of via the Witch, is powerful and controlling, as she is able to administer life-altering punishments in response to her daughter's accidental disobedience. Because the Witch's mother's garden was pilfered by the Baker's father, the Baker is rendered impotent and the Witch made effectually so, through the disfigurement.

Once the spell is broken and the Witch is returned to her original physical state, she, like the others whose wishes have been granted, believes she will be happy. For her, that means a return to a relationship with Rapunzel, but that is not to be. At the beginning of Act 2, she sings, "I was perfect/ I had everything but beauty/ I had power/ And a daughter like a flower/ In a tower / Then I went into the woods/

To get my wish / And I'm ordinary / Lost my power and my flower"
(Sondheim, 1987). The Witch realizes that in her quest for beauty, she
lost her daughter, as she was too preoccupied with the Baker's quest to
keep her daughter "safe." Still, her part of the "Act II Prologue," the
Witch is focused on herself and her needs in relationship to her daughter. Not until "Lament," does Sondheim give and the audience understand a new aspect of the overbearing mother. The Witch's lament here
is for her daughter's death, at the foot of the giant, seeking to avenge
her husband's death. She questions, "How could I / Have shielded you
from her? / Or them?" (Sondheim, 1987). She realizes that no amount
of overbearing protection could have saved her daughter from her fate;
"No matter what you say / Children won't listen. / No matter what you
know / Children refuse to learn / Guide them along the way / Still they
won't listen / Children can only grow / From something you love / To
something you lose" (Sondheim, 1987). With Rapunzel dead, the lesson
and potential for change are left for the mother, not the daughter. She
struggles to find meaning, as the audience comes to have enormous pity
for her. She is not simply a mother who locked her daughter in a tower,
but one who tried with most extreme measures to protect the thing most
precious to her, the beautiful, refined naïve projection of herself. The
Witch's actions have all been attempts to keep pure the narcissistic projection of self. It is an example of a most extreme insularity.

In "Last Midnight," when the other in the woods refuses to allow
her to take revenge on Jack, who she blames for Rapunzel's death, she
tries an opposite strategy. Those still alive in the woods: the Baker, Little
Red, Cinderella, and Jack have banded together. The Witch wants the
others to turn Jack over to her and when they will not she attempts to
break them all apart singing, "I'm leaving you alone/ You can tend the
garden it's yours / Separate and alone." Her overbearing nature has
been broken. She will no longer attempt to impose her will on others;
she will not seek a substitute daughter figure or transfer her dominance.
She requests of her mother, another witch the audience never sees, to
return her ugliness. It was when she was ugly that she had a connection
with her daughter, so a return to that state is an attempt to regain the
all that she has lost, both her power and her love. The Witch's mother,
however, does not grant her wish. The Witch begs, "Give me claws and
a hunch / Just away from this bunch" (Sondheim, 1987); instead, she
disappears completely from the stage. Nothing can be reversed. The
Witch's overbearing nature crushed her daughter, and in that collapse,

she lost her identity. In part, the Witch's attraction to Rapunzel has been Rapunzel's ability to perfect that which the Witch wanted to be. It is the opposite of the attractive to inferiority that Klein describes. Instead, the Witch has sought the externalized perfection of her daughter. The Witch's particular form of overbearingness is a reaction formation against her own insecurity and to fulfill her desire to control the external locus of her definition of self. Rapunzel then sublimates her aggression against her mother, through dalliance with the prince, after her mother banishes her. Just as the Witch allowed her beauty to be stolen by her mother when she allowed the Baker's father to ravage her garden, not symbolically speaking, the Witch cuts Rapunzel's hair and banishes her after she allows the prince into her tower. Later, when the audience sees her again, she is a beggar woman, wandering the woods with twin infants and is found by her prince, but is soon abandoned by him as he finds a new princess to arouse his lust. Lost and crazed, she becomes an easy but accidental casualty of the giant.

Her mother's overbearing nature has left her vulnerable to all the forces that can prey on her in the woods. There is also an interesting switching of sexual roles that takes place between this mother and daughter. When the Witch is ugly and Rapunzel is young and beautiful, the Witch feels the need to foreclose on Rapunzel's potential sexuality by locking her in the tower, instead of using her as an access point for the desire of the Other. By the time the Witch regains her physical beauty, Rapunzel has been robbed of hers, by her mother, as a means of punishment for allowing the prince to visit. Only one of the pair can be a sexual object while the other physically denigrated. The more the alternate roles, the more the power of their sexuality is diminished overall. Finally, one is dead and the other invisible. The overbearing mother has destroyed both her daughter and herself.

Next to Normal is a show with an interesting mix of absent mother, as Diana is for Natalie, and overbearing mother, as Diana is for Gabe. The overbearing relationship between Diana and Gabe is beyond atypical. Until the middle of Act 1, when Diana emerges during a dinner party with Natalie's new boyfriend, with a birthday cake for her dead son, does the audience learn that her son is, in fact, dead. Until that point, the audience fully believes that Gabe is living teenage boy, doted on by his loving mother, despised by his younger sister. Due to brilliant acting and staging, the musical's secret is truly kept until "He's Not Here," when Dan gently sings to his wife, "He's been dead / Sixteen years / No, my love / He's not here" (Yorkey, 2009). Diana's response is the passionate, angry, "You Don't Know," in which she describes her life without Gabe as "When the world that once had color / Fades to white and grey and black" (Yorkey, 2009).

Being bipolar for Diana in this show means a colorless existence. It also means she is a different mother to each of her children. As discussed in Chapter 2, Diana is functionally absent as mother to Natalie, but for Gabe she is overbearing. It is crucial to remember that while Gabe is dead, his presence is very alive to Diana and by associate to the rest of the family. It seems almost too easy an analysis to claim that Diana's overbearing behavior toward Gabe is the result of his illness as an infant. In "Aftershocks," Gabe, in erased in her memory by a series of ETC treatments, returns, perceived intangibly by Diana and sings; "They've managed to get rid of me / I'm gone without a trace. / But sear the soul and leave a scar / No treatment can erase / They cut away the cancer / But forgot to fill the hole. / They moved me from your memory / I'm still there in your soul" (Yorkey, 2009). She struggles to remember, to fight against the ETC until "How Could I Even Forget," when, in a round format with Dan, she recalls the details of Gabe's illness and trip to the hospital. Her memory is straightforward and brutal; "Someone simply said, / Your child is ..." (Yorkey, 2009). Neither she nor Dan can utter the word dead. For Dan, it is the pain of loss that prevents him from singing it. For Diana, it is because Gabe has never truly died. His literal death has become a somewhat sinister omnipresence in her mind making him more alive than dead for her.

Gabe's insistent solo "I'm Alive" with driving electric guitar and solid rock foundation makes the point that his presence is tempting and ominous, much like the experience of bipolar disorder itself. Gabe sings, "I'm what you want me to be / I'm your worst fear / You'll find it in me. / Come closer (2x)./ I'm more than memory / I am what might be/ I am mystery/ You know me./ So show me" (Yorkey, 2009). Gabe's sensuous and unrelenting temptation here also defines them both; he reminds, "And I need you to need me / It's no surprise" (Yorkey, 2009). The codependency of the relationship, even though internalized and projected outward, is overwhelming and dangerous. Gabe tells Diana, or really Diana tells herself, as Gabe is actually the Id of her unstable mind, "I'll burn you. / I'll heal you" (Yorkey, 2009). The maternal love that Diana has for her dead child, at the sake of her living one, is more than guilt. It is a reversal of the overbearing maternal relationship. In her psychosis, she has reabsorbed her child, an ultimate act of overbearing and narcissistic maternal love. He is so much a part of her that she cannot let go, even when he dies. The maternal narcissism is too strong.

Importantly, Gabe in the show dies at 18 months old, a significant age for infantile psychosexual development, the age at which for Lacan, the child begins to separate from the mother, at the beginning of the mirror stage. The mirror stage, as Lacan describes with great depth in *Ecrits*, is the " … particular function of imagos, which is to establish a relationship between and organism and its reality – or, as they say between the *Innenwelt* and the *Umwelt*." Lacan wants to draw the distinction between a subject's interior life, or Imaginary stage and their external environment, which will help to form the exterior of the Symbolic for that same subject. For Diana, Gabe is both her innenwelt and her umwelt, as her disease has eliminated the distinction between the two. Since that destruction occurred at the very stage when the separation should have happened, it makes the bond between the mother and child, even more significant. As the mother of a living child, Diana never experienced the natural separation that would occur with her son as he enters the mirror stage, Gabe, even as she imagines him maturing, will always be her infant son.

Both Melanie Klein and Jacque Lacan describe a sort of bubble or enclosure that is the fantasy of the womb surrounding the child. When the child is alive, the child must use the aggressive tendencies Riviere theorizes to cut through the enclosure. When the child is dead, the enclosure looks more like Kristeva's description of Michelangelo's *Pieta*, in which the living mother is left devastated to encapsulate her son's body. Like the Christian myth, the son is resurrected, but here it is to Diana's detriment. As Diana resurrects her son, she gives herself the ability to be the overbearing mother that she did not have the chance to be. In part, both she and Dan blame themselves for Gabe's death. They were young; they didn't understand his constant crying; they didn't get challenge doctors forcefully enough, seek enough opinions, or get him to the hospital soon enough the night of his death, at least in their memories, which is their reality. For a mother whose mental health was already unstable, this is the breaking point. The guilt, combined with a natural predisposition for being boisterous bossiness, perhaps related to her mania, creates the perfect conditions for her to enact her own overbearing tendencies on herself. For Diana, that overbearing nature is exacted on herself, as punishment. She does not choose her daughter as a target because her daughter, as she reminds both Natalie and herself, was born to alleviate the grief she feels, but she doesn't really want that grief alleviated. She wants to hold on it, to hold it like a child itself. Gabe is a projection of her grief, and her overbearing nature is the way that she holds on to that grief. It is an anti-abjection mechanism. Instead of ridding herself of the material which causes her pain, she reclaims it. As an overbearing mother, par excellence, she takes in the entirety of the abject, the dead son, and makes him the most essential part of who she is. No amount of therapy or human connection and interaction can trump that. Even when she leaves, Diana is not leaving only to give her daughter a chance to live, but to give herself more time with her son/self.

Next to Normal is the most daring and honest portrayal of a maternal figure in musical theatre in the twenty-first century. The Prom had similar potential, even though written as a musical comedy instead of drama, but it fails. The Prom, which made its Broadway debut in 2018, lost its 2019 bid for Best Musical at the Tony Awards in 2019 for good reason. It is the story of four faded and jaded Broadway actors searching for a cause to make themselves relevant again, when they find the story of Emma, a lesbian teenager in Middle America whose prom has been canceled by her school district because she wants to take a girl as her date. The four actors arrive in town, antics and a predictable poignancy ensue, as the prom is supposedly back on, with the promise of Emma escorting Alyssa, the closeted daughter of the close-minded PTA president. On prom night, Emma arrives to find alone at a fake prom, as required by law, while the rest of the school is at the real prom across town. With tears and expected hijinks, an actual prom comes to fruition; Alyssa comes out to her mom and attends the prom with Emma where the two finally kiss. As Broadway musicals have become increasingly socially aware and have been written with young adult audiences in mind, a musical about homosexuality and teenagers seems almost long overdue. The Prom is important because it dares to focus on these issues, but it lacks real depth, as if it is a musical afraid to be itself. Classical comedy is the root of musical theatre. Countless musicals of the Golden Age end with actual marriage, proposals of marriage or at least, a happy romantic union. The Prom is no different. The kiss at the end is what the audience dreams is the beginning of a happy relationship for Emma and Alyssa. Ending their relationship, as many other Broadway relationships end, beautifully normalizes the romance, but what is missing is complexity surrounding that resolution.

From the musical's beginning, the audience knows that Emma's parents are accepting of her sexuality and supportive in her desire to attend prom with a same-sex partner. While this is not always the side of teenage homosexuality shown, there are understanding parents and it is important to show all potential relationships in drama, even positive ones. The problem lies in the relationship between Alyssa and her mother. Mrs. Greene is the pushy, perfect president of the PTA. She advocates against Emma's right to have a same-sex partner at the prom, never imagining that same-sex partner is her daughter. Mrs. Greene, in response to the ruling the school must hold its prom as planned in its gym, orchestrates another prom, at an outside venue. The audience gets a bit of reality at the beginning of Act 2, when Emma and Alyssa break up, after the prom night gone wrong. Alyssa explains, "You know what my mother is like. She's a complete and total control freak" (Beguelin, 2018). In language that sounds very much like a teenage girl, Alyssa is saying her mother is stereotypically overbearing, as she sings, "The hair has to be perfect. / The As have to be straight" (Beguelin, 2018). Of course, implied in that line is that everything about her daughter has to be straight. Mrs. Greene can imagine nothing different. Such lack of imagination is a quintessential component of overbearing motherhood. When a mother is overbearing, as Mrs. Greene is, she can only imagine her daughter as a diluted version of herself. It is a variation of the theme of inferiority that Riviere identifies. The overbearing mother cannot handle a true rival, and so she projects an image of her daughter that is not quite as "successful" as she is, allowing the mother the power to mold that daughter into her image. It is a Pygmalion-like strategy that is bound to backfire. "Alyssa Greene" goes on to detail the ways in which Alyssa is supposed to be perfect according to her mother's standards; "Endless rules apply when you're Alyssa Green." The song transcends the plight of a young lesbian woman longing to reveal her sexual identity. It is the plea of any, perhaps every teenager who feels oppressed by her parents' desires and their particular mechanisms for normalization, in whatever way that is defined by them. Alyssa sings softly, "And you wish there was a world / Where you were simply free to live / And when people criticized you / You had no more shits to give" (Beguelin, 2018). The song is about her mother's controlling nature, but also about the controlling nature of her community and her society at large addressing more a moment, in a very real way, the societal oppression that underscores the entire plot. Alyssa wants not to care about her mother's demands, but she does care and she is torn by her simultaneous desires.

Those desires are compounded by the profound feeling she has that her mother is using her as a pawn to regain her father's love; "'Cause mom's convinced if you're perfect / You're father might come back" (Beguelin, 2018). The traditional marital relationship and family structure are at stake here, and Alyssa's sexuality flouts not only her mother's definition of perfect, but that familial structure itself.

The song ends with Alyssa's lament sung before and after Emma leaves; "You're not yourself. / You're not what she wants. / You're someone in between. / Your whole life's a lie when you're Alyssa Green" (Beguelin, 2018). This profound declaration should be heartbreaking for the audience. The "in-between" state in which Alyssa lives is one in which she cannot be comfortable either living with the intense drive for perfect and hetero-normativity that her mother demands, or the closeted relationship she has with Emma. Mrs. Greene has displayed what Klein explains is a love of power. As a defense against the loss of omnipotence, here that the mother has exerted over the daughter, the mother tried to implement a new form of control; "One way of reaching security is by aiming at omnipotent power in order to control all potentially painful conditions, and have access to all useful, desirable things, both within oneself and without. In phantasy, omnipotence shall bring security" (39). With Mr. Greene's departure, Mrs. Greene has experienced a decline in her sense of power and security. She imposes her rules on Alyssa to try to regain that sense of well-being, but those rules comprise Alyssa's own psychological security.

With such a poignant and real struggle articulated, Mrs. Greene's acceptance of Alyssa's sexuality at the end of the musical seems too contrived. While she is, at first, reluctant to accept her daughter's coming out, she does so, rather quickly when Barry confronts her with the possibility that she will lose Alyssa completely. While this may be true, and while Barry is the most developed and nuanced characters of the four actors who have come to town to save the prom, Barry is still a comedic figure and the scene is under-developed. The happy ending is too easy; no mother that overbearing and bigoted would change her mind so quickly. While the outcome is positive for Alyssa, who gets to be herself and also positive for Mrs. Greene who has suspended her overbearing nature, it is not realistic. If Broadway in 1959 could show a realistic outcome for an overbearing mother, it should be able to do as well in 2019.

CHAPTER 4

The Inconsequential Mother

Abstract This chapter will explore musicals in which there is an expectation that mother figures will play a larger role in the actual stage performance than they do. Such incongruity of expectation and presentation not only challenges audiences' expectations, but also demonstrates some movement in changing conventions. These barely there mother figures are significant in the potential they could possess or the lack they leave in character and audience through their minimal, but intriguing presence. The chapter provides analysis of such figures in *Passing Strange, The 25th Annual Putnam County Spelling Bee, Fun Home*, and *Dear Evan Hansen*. This figure is the one who offers the greatest freedom from convention, as neither she, nor her children are forced into stereotype.

Keywords Inconsequential · Other · Transference · Symbolic · Jouissance

Stereotypical expectations tell audiences and society alike that a mother figure, whether present or absent, should be a figure of great consequence in the life of her child. It should be her wisdom and love that informs the child's good behavior or her lack thereof which ruins the child. In some tales of triumph over adversity, the mother figure, in her grand failure, can be the main obstacle which a child overcomes.

© The Author(s) 2019   55
G. M. MacKenzie, *Maternal Representations in Twenty-First Century Broadway Musicals*, Pivotal Studies in the Global American Literary Imagination, https://doi.org/10.1007/978-3-030-32337-0_4

These conventional expectations, or any conventions as Blau Duplessis articulates, are "... like a 'script,' which suggests sequences of action and response, the meaning we give these, and ways of organizing experience by choices, emphases, priorities" (2). She goes on to explain, "[S]o too literature as human institution is, baldly, organized by many ideological scripts. Any literary convention – plots, narrative sequences, characters in bit parts – as an instrument that claims to depict experience, also interprets it. No convention is neutral, purely mimetic or purely aesthetic" (Blau Duplessis, 2). The scripts society provides to us are those from which many work to create art. In this view, conventions are largely the object itself and art is the mimicry of that. To use Lacanian terminology, the convention is the Big Other, with the work of art most particularly the musical production, the petit objet a.

In the Lacanian lexicon, the Big Other frequently takes the form of society as passed down through paternal lineage so that it is the traditional figure which gives us language and the law. The petit objet a is the figure which looks to that Other and reflects it back with an ironically narcissistic inferiority complex. Kristeva moves from this imaginary mirror-image stalemate to a more freeing position for women, especially mothers, in the concept of la langue. La langue, the insular communication established by and unique to a mother/child dyad, is incomprehensible outside of that pair. It both predates and defies the rules and order of the language of the patriarchy. In theatrical terms, it is linked, according to Kristeva, one of the six most essential elements of tragic composition, language. In *Poetics*, Aristotle speaks of rhythm as the most important component of language in a play, as through rhythm the speaker, and audience via catharsis, reach an orgasmic purity, not unlike Lacan's jouissance. As Kristeva points out, "[R]hythm and song hence arouse the impure, the other of mind, the passionate-corporeal-sexual-viral, but they harmonize it, arrange it differently than the wise man's knowledge does" (Powers of Horror, 28). That song, "[V]ocal and muscular contractions, spasms of the glottis and motor system – all make up for the absence of intrauterine life components" (Desire in Language, 282). If we look at these two factors of Kristevean thought together, its seems to indicate that music should give the opportunity for expression of the intensity of the maternal connection and that music has, at its core, the fraught intimacy of the mother/child dyad. It can also be the representation of the loss of that maternal connection.

In "Stabat Mater," Kristeva's very personal account of motherhood, she claims, "A mother's identity survives only thanks to the well-known fact that consciousness is lulled by habit, wherein a woman protects herself along the frontier that divides her body and make an expatriate of her child" (146). That frontier is the also the plausible dividing line between song and speech or between the semiotic, pre-linguistic bond between the mother and child, and the symbolic, or language structures of the patriarchal order. The line that divides the maternal part of the mothering subject from her pre-maternal self is often assumed, to be one which the woman wishes to have blurred. Such blurring or oblite-ration of the pre-maternal self is the demand of conventional society and silence surrounding that demand is expected. As Kristeva theorizes, "Nor is there any less silence concerning the mental and physical suffering associated with childbirth and, even more, with the self-denial implicit in making oneself anonymous in order to transit social norms with one may disavow for oneself but which *one must* pass on to the child, whose education is a link to generations past. But, with the ambivalence char-acteristic of masochism, this suffering goes hand in hand with jubila-tion whereby a woman ordinarily averse to perversion allows herself to engage in 'coded' perversity, a perversity that is absolutely fundamental, the ultimate basis of all social life, without which society would be una-ble to reproduce itself or maintain its notion of a normative household" ("Stabat Mater", 149–150).

It seems reasonable to postulate that any commercial venue, as an agent of societal norms, is one which seeks to uphold this maternal fal-lacy. Broadway, as the most commercial arm of American theatre, would then follow that pattern and choose to stage productions which also uphold those myths, but musical theatre, even more than drama, is an agent of subversion in the guise of conventional normativity. As Scott McMillian points out, much of musical theatre is based on the difference between reality and expectation. This is a frequent criticism of the form, as casual audience members will comment that gangsters don't sing in the middle of a craps games and characters don't step out of painting to give elaborate recitative. In musicals they do, and that brings the audience type of cathartic joy and appreciation of the irony of the situ-ation. Motherhood also can bring a similar type of ironic joy, as Kristeva demonstrates, but to make a neat equation is far too simple. Musical the-atre itself is assuming the role of the mother for the audience, but it is staging mothers, just not in the range of possibilities that motherhood can present. Of course, this argument is built on the premise that theatre itself is a mimetic art and that argument is the foundation upon which this particular text is built.

If that is true, then musical theatre should present a myriad of maternal images, but it does not. Musical theatre in the twenty-first century forecloses on its own potential and limits the images it presents. As already discussed, some of the most common images are those of the overbearing mother and the absent mother. These conventional images play with the basic Freudian divide of the differences between being a mother to a girl and being the mother to a boy. As Kristeva explains Freud, "The mother of a son (henceforth the generic 'infant' no longer exists) is a *being* confronted with a *being-for-him*. The mother of a daughter replays in reverse the encounter with her own mother: differential or leveling of beings, glimpses of oneness or paranoid primary identification phantasized a primordial substance" (Desire in Language, 279). The absent mother figure can be understood as the mother of a son, since there, the mother sacrifices her identity for that of her child. She is missing because she is no longer relevant as a being of her own. The overbearing mother can be understood as the mother of a daughter whose insistent presence is an attempt to gain back her own identity that is deflated by the birth of her daughter.

The inconsequential mother is neither of those. She is not lost in the figure of her son, nor looming large over the figure of her daughter. She is simply not as relevant in their lives, nor are her children as relevant in her life, as the audience expects. This figure is emerging increasingly on the Broadway musical stage and offers much to explore. In particular, *The 25th Annual Putnam County Spelling Bee, Passing Strange, Fun Home,* and *Dear Evan Hanson* present this mother figure.

From the audience's first introductions to the main spellers in *The 25th Annual Putnam County Spelling Bee,* the expectation is set that parents, especially mothers, do not, for the most part, figure prominently into the lives of these children. *The 25th Annual Putnam County Spelling Bee,* which won two Tony Awards in 2005, after coming to Broadway from an enormously successful run off-Broadway, is the story of the participants in a spelling bee, whose winner gets to participate in the National Spelling Bee. The pre-teen participants, three boys and three girls, compete for success while navigating their personal histories and interpersonal relationships. The show employs both physical and improvisational comedy, along with a large degree of audience participation to achieve an atmosphere that feels very much like the interior workings of a twelve-year-old mind. It is brilliant, hilarious, and poignant. From the very beginning, when the audience first encounters the spellers, it is evident that their parents, for the most part, are not huge influences in their lives. The sole exception, Olive, who longs for her mother's love and attention, helps to establish this book's conception of the absent mother. In the show's opening song, Chip, the most savvy speller of the group sings, "... my parents keep on telling me, just being here is winning. Although I know it isn't so" (1). Chip recognizes that his parents' words are trite attempts to quell any anxiety he might have over competition and/or an attempt to prove their unconditional love. He knows those clichéd efforts are meaningless and sets forth his own agenda. Here, it is the use of language that highlights the lack of relevance. This level of communication is subsequent to the semiotic chora; it is symbolic language, in Kristevean terminology, that which is used after the bond of the mother and child is broken. It is simply language, imposed by the patriarchal order to impose order. Since the message is sent in words, and not in sound or touch, the key components of communication in the mother/child bond reliance on the mother alone in already broken. Once that bond has started to decay, the child can start to escape from its confines, as Chip does when he says that he knows the truth his parents are trying to mediate. Recognizing the façade that parents or a mother can construct helps to show the child that conventional notions of motherhood itself are societal constructs. One the child sees the construct, the power of that construct is deflated, making the mother/child bond inconsequential and allowing the child to be self-reliant. Chip can choose for himself then to what degree he wants to try to succeed.

Olive's parents, as absent, do not try to intervene in her choices. Their absenteeism is her defining characteristic and the absence, particularly of her mother, is what binds and drives her through most of the play. There is one moment, however, again at the very beginning of the show, when Olive shows that she has some understanding of her mother's inconsequential place in her life. The audience learns, at the start, that there is a twenty-five dollar entrance fee for all contestants; Olive's parents have neglected to pay the fee. There is no indication that financial hardship has prevented payment; the implication is that they have simply not bothered. When asked how she arrived at the bee, Olive responds that she took the bus. Even while she longs for her absent mother, on some level, she has already rendered her inconsequential. Olive wants to participate in the spelling bee; her mother is in India and her father is working, so she finds a way to patriate on her own. She has found her own drive. The inconsequential role that her mother chooses to play, while condemned by most audience members who feel pity for the poor little girls with no parental involvement, has actually given Olive the survival skills that she needs to grow into a successful adult.

The musical's "Epilogues" prove this as the audience learns, "Olive Ostrovsky went home to an empty house, an uncertain future, and a well-worn dictionary – but with a strange new conviction that she would be able to face all three. She grew up to be a loving and attentive parent – and the host of her own radio show, where every year, she interviewed the runner up of the Putnam County spelling bee" (Finn and Sheinkin, 31). Olive is able to survive being the runner-up of the spelling bee, because she allows her mother, by the last round of the bee, to become inconsequential. Olive conquers, but the epilogue cannot let the audience see that alone and cannot abandon traditional notions of motherhood. Instead, the audience learns that Olive grows up to be the opposite of her mother—"loving and attentive." It begs the audience to question though, whether Olive's children will have her same level of determination and self-reliance.

Youth, the protagonist of *Passing Strange*, is self-possessed from the start. *Passing Strange* had a rather short-lived run on Broadway, opening on February 28, 2008, and closing on July 20, 2008, but in that short time, the musical enjoyed critical acclaim, was nominated for seven Tony Awards, and earned one for Best Book of a Musical. With book, music and lyrics by Stew and Heidi Rodewald, the musical focuses on the life of a young African-American man who leaves the safety and tradition of his middle class, religious life in Los Angeles for adventure in Amsterdam and Berlin and something he calls, "the real."

That term, the real, is reminiscent of Lacan's register, the Real, which is characterized as the most intense experience of simultaneous pleasure and pain a subject can undergo. For Lacan, this experience is marked by a process of self-nomination or purposeful rejection of society's norms and hierarchies. Interestingly, in *The Four Fundamental Concepts of Psychoanalysis*, Lacan states that "… neurosis recreates a harmony with the real – a real that may well not be determined" (22). For a musical theatre piece, the use of the word harmony here is most remarkable as harmony is the layers of two related sounds against each other to produce a duality of sound that many listeners claim is more fully realized than a single note. Harmony with the real might then be the achieving a duality of subjectivity in which one can both know the real and still interact with society. To elucidate that process, we have Lacan's claim that "[T]he real supports the phantasy, the phantasy protects the real" (*Four Fundamentals*, 41). This relationship is akin to that of the mother/child dyad; the phantasy is the cocoon-like symbiosis of the child in the womb and just after birth, when there is total insular dependence by the child on the mother for basic life needs and the mother on the child for psychological stability through her new definition of self. Having experienced the real, the child recognizing the harmonic phantasy, but supports it, nonetheless, because without that experience as a starting point from which to free oneself, there could be no real. The codependency of the mother/child mimics that of the phantasy/real. When the symbiosis of that dyad is broken or weak from inception, the mother figure, by either her choice, her child's choice, or both, is rendered inconsequential and each can begin a journey toward real independence.

Passing Strange enacts that interplay between the mother and the child that both intersects with the real and defines a version of inconsequential mothering that is generative for both parties, playing against the connotation of that term. The first interactions the audience sees between Mother and Youth in *Passing Strange* center around Youth's avoidance of church. Mother wants Youth not only to attend church services but also to blend in but looking and behaving like everyone else in the congregation. As Youth acquiesces and attends the service, Mother prays for more begging, "Lord ... show up and save him this morning. Show him you are real" (Rodewald, 8). The Mother, already realizing that she is inconsequential in her son's life, prays for another figure to take her place, here the father figure in the form of god. Youth doesn't care about finding god, but recognizes that there is a lack, in Lacanian terminology, a gateway to the real, that needs to be filled. Here begins Youth's journey to fill the lack through music. As narrator sings, "I think the Real's gettin' involved" (Rodewald, 9) in response to the church music, the Youth starts to feel music is his means of escape. He cries, "This is real" (Rodewald, 9) in response to the music alone, in the face of his mother's great disappointment.

What follows this revelation and disappointment is a traditionally structured call and response section between Reverend Jones and the choir, in which Reverend Jones asks of God is in fact real and if the choir can, in fact, "deal" with God being real. The choir answers excitedly in the affirmative, which asserts the primacy of the God/father figure, even the reverend here, in place of the mother. Both Mother and Youth witness this moment which signifies the beginning of Youth's journey away from Mother and her gradual loss of relevance in his life.

Instead of leaving the church and Mother completely though, Youth does the unexpected and joins the choir, for the musical, not religious real. In the choir, Youth finds Edwina, the object of his sexual attraction. Edwina takes the place Mother, as sex object replaces maternal object in Youth's consciousness, signifying a maturation that again renders Mother inconsequential to some degree. As Mother's potency fades, Youth gains greater ability to pursue his real.

Shortly thereafter, Youth leaves for Amsterdam to find his real and "Mom Song" follows. The omission of the possessive in the title suggests that this song is not specific to the relationship of these two people, but is characteristic of mother/child relationships in general. First, Mother questions, "I'm hardly afraid / Of your new world's strange design. / Why don't you make room for me, / As I made room for you in mine?" (Rodewald, 34). Mother expresses the expectation that the mother/child dyad is reciprocal, and is hurt that, for her, it is not. She goes on to sing, "See, I've been running from this world, / For far longer than you. / But I didn't know where else to go, / So I hid from it in you. / And then, for a time, / This world was yours and mine, / And that was only yesterday, you see, / But now you've got your own thing / And it does not include me" (Rodewald, 34). This heartbreaking lyric is a melodic retelling of Kristeva's "Stabat Mater," in which she articulates the "... *relationship* between her and us, an idealization of primary narcissism" (133). The "her and us" in Kristeva is the mother and child; the idealization being that for the mother, the child is a beautiful and perfection extension of the self, one that produces "... the *consecrated* (religious or secular) representation of femininity [that] is subsumed under maternity" (Kristeva, 133). In *Passing Strange*, Mother assumes that Youth will perfect her shortcomings and stay with her in the protected nest she has created out of her own fear. She built her life for him and is not devastated that his architecture does not have space for her. She feels rendered inconsequential and spends the rest of the musical trying to gain back relevance even as her son grows without her.

4 THE INCONSEQUENTIAL MOTHER   63

The scene that follows "Mom Song" also offers a single line brimming with meaning in this context. As Mother and Youth battle over his attempts to leave Los Angeles, Mother proclaims, in response to her son, "Joy is for children" (Rodewald, 36). If that is true, then in the perspective of the mother, the son's leaving forecloses her quest for the real, via the experience of jouissance, literally translated as "joy," but for Lacan more like ecstasy. The mother's fear of losing her child is not then fear of losing the symbiosis established by the early infantile bond, but is fear of the ability to escape that relationship herself. The great irony, here, it seems, is that for the child to leave to pursue his own real, the mother most forgo her willingness to do the same. Motherhood and adulthood are positions so enmeshed in the rules of society that there can be no joy; there can be no real. That is the true pain of birth.

Youth has a glimmer of the realization of that pain, when he sings, "She's living in a phony paradise .../ No wait, .../ So many things she doesn't realize ... / She's ... basking in hell's ... sunshine ..." (Rodewald, 51). Youth perceives that the world in which his mother lives is a façade of joy, not joy itself, but he doesn't think that she understands that too. The underestimation of the mother by the child is false, but is also what helps in the process of rendering the mother inconsequential. When the mother truly is irrelevant, or under-relevant in the child's life, then both can begin the process of independence or the move to the real that both desire.

Such lack of consequence is found in "Mom Phone Call" near the end of Act 2. Mother asks typically banal questions of her son, such as "Did that jacket I sent fit alright?" (Rodewald, 86). This small talk with no real meaning attached to it represents a break in the bond of the semiotic that according to Kristeva is the pre-linguistic bodily connection between mother and child. Here, Mother and Youth have been physically separated for a long time, and that physical separation has led to a degeneration of the emotional bond they once had. Practically speaking, Mother has lost physical contact with Youth to the extent that she doesn't know what clothes will fit him. She longs to talk with him about, " ...important things ..." (Rodewald, 87) and he reiterates, "Mom, I live here now" (Rodewald, 87) cementing the semiotic break. Not only are the pair separated by space, they are separated by the perception. The separation gives each a chance to self-define, but while the Youth is eager to do so, Mother shows no desire to be accepted that position. She questions, "Why do you need a particular place to be yourself? Can't you be yourself at home?" (Rodewald, 88). The answer is whole-heartedly no. Youth or any child needs a physical separation from the maternal bond to be able to develop a sense of self to get to the real. Mother believes that home is where she is able to define herself, but only when Youth is present too. What Mother fails to recognize is she also cannot define herself while home. Home has been created for her, as it is created for most mothers in society, by society itself acting in the position of the patriarchy. In *Passing Strange*, as in many facets of twenty-first-century life, that role is played by the church. Until the home is a place where the mother/woman can define herself and not assume the definitions of others, then her real cannot be achieved there either.

There is a glimmer of realization in last moments of the play, when Mother sings, "Don't be sad about your chosen path, / And where it's taken you thus far. / Cuz this is what you did, / And that is who you are. / And it's alright" (Rodewald, 100). In the end, Mother finally gives Youth permission, after he has left and established his own path, to do so. This permission is not, in fact, for Youth, but for herself, **to** in relief, be able to accept what he has chosen and, in relief, to be able to accept herself for accepting the separation. While Mother makes no attempt to forge her own path, simply acknowledging that her son is gone and for the first time, not trying to bring him back or impose something upon him from afar, she is rendering herself in a way, inconsequential. While the narrator asks her, "Is it alright?" her response, repeatedly, is "Yes, it's alright ..." (Rodewald, 100). While she responds to the question with a statement, the ellipsis provides a type of condition, an implied questioning of the conviction under the statement. That makes her inconsequential for herself, but her son is not fully inconsequential to her. She is on a path to an imaginary world, while her son can hopefully make it to the real.

In *Fun Home*, the 2015 Tony Award winning collaboration among Alison Bechdel, Jeanine Tesori and Lisa Kron, the audience is uncertain if either Alison or her father, Bruce reach the real. It is obvious, though, that her mother Helen is barred from that, not because she is inconsequential in her daughter's life, but because she is inconsequential in her own. *Fun Home* is an adaptation of Alison Bechdel's graphic memoir of the same name. It chronicles Bechdel's childhood and young adult life especially as she related to her father, Bruce. The story, really a musical memory play, traces Alison's childhood with her father who was both a high school English teacher and the local mortician. While her father works to feminize his daughter, who longs to dress like her brothers, he also pursues sexual relationships with young, sometimes underage men. When Alison arrives at Oberlin College, she meets Jane, quickly realizes that she is lesbian and writes home to both parents to tell them of her realization. Though concerned at her parents' lack of response to this revelation, she brings Jane home with her for Thanksgiving Break, where both are accepted and when she learns not only that her father is gay, but also that her mother has known of his dalliances throughout their marriage. She tries to reconnect with her father, to discuss their shared and ironically open secret, but the conversation never really begins. She returns to school and her father steps in front of a truck to commit suicide.

The musical is book-ended with Alison recounting her desire to play airplane with her father. Her desire, as finely articulated in the last moment of the play is not just to "Fly / Up so high / I can see all of Pennsylvania" (Kron, 2015), but to find her identity by rising above him, not by remaining under his will. Her last words are, "Every so often there was a rare moment of perfect balance when I soared above him" (Kron, 2015). The simultaneously dominant and aloof personality of her father, baffled Alison as a child and dominated her curiosity as an adult, but mostly missing from that process was her mother, Helen. This is highly unusual for a play centered on a parent/child relationship, as conventionally, the same-sex parent is the one with which the child has the most fraught relationship. It would be easy to make the claim that Alison's relationship with her father is more compelling because they are both homosexual, but that would be to make the assumption that sexual preference is the dominating bond that links parent/child, which is not a claim I am making. Instead, I would argue that the relationship between Alison and her mother, albeit given less plot space, is no less compelling.

The first encounter the audience has with Helen is in "Welcome to Our House on Maple Avenue." In this song, Helen and Alison are detached from each other; their only relationship is their shared desire to please Bruce and maintain their façade of normalcy in front of the representative from Allegheny Historical Society, coming to examine their house. Both mother and daughter aim to please husband/father even as they question what he wants from this visit. Helen repeatedly sings, "He wants – / He wants – / He wants – " (Kron, 2015), but does not ask or show concern for what her pre-teen children may want. His needs, not hers or her daughter's, dominate her thoughts and actions in this early scene. Mother and daughter do not interact in any meaningful way, both showing Alison's relationship with her mother is fairly and unusually superficial and that such an inconsequential relationship with her mother has left Alison with the ability to bond with her father more.

"Helen's Etude" demonstrates, profoundly, how inconsequential she is in her family's life. While Bruce seduces Roy in the main parlor, Helen practices the piano and shoes away Alison with her childish questions about Chopin and her not-so-childish statement, "I like Roy. He's funny" (Kron, 2015). Whether totally innocent or stated with keen observation that Alison's childhood psyche isn't ready to understand, that statement is too much for Helen to bare. She retreats to her music, ignoring her daughter while providing the soundtrack for her husband's love affair. She makes no effort to engage with her daughter or to consciously consider her husband's infidelity in any way. She could express anger, hurt, fear, or forgiveness, but chooses to express nothing. She renders herself inconsequential in her own life, setting an example for her daughter that she too should linger in the wings instead of taking the center of her own life. Because Helen is inconsequential though, the example she sets also lacks consequence, which is positive for Alison, as she does put her needs forward.

When Helen does try to intercede on her daughter's behalf, to allow Alison to express herself instead of cowing to her father's dominance, Alison does not accept the intercession and defends her father, even as the defense undermines her own will. This is the scenario that occurs in "I Leapt Out of the Closet" which begins with Alison juxtaposing her outing with her father's suicide and ends with her story of a class geography assignment. In the scene, Young Alison explains, "In school we're learning maps and globes, and Miss Windsor said draw a map of all the places people in our family have been too" (Kron, 2015). Alison's map is very interpretive, and when she shows her father, he demands a more literal rendering of the geography; "Alison, this is how it should be" (Kron, 2015) he states, while she responds, "But I like the way mine was" (Kron, 2015). Alison is willing to challenge her father until her mother steps in with, "Bruce, it's a drawing. It doesn't matter" (Kron, 2015). His emotional response prompts Alison to backtrack, claiming, "No. I like the one you did, Daddy" (Kron, 2015). Even in her desire to defend her daughter's autonomy and creativity, Helen is ignored. The mother/child bond is virtually none existent and that, for Alison, allows her to be free, which it gives Helen nothing to be at all.

Even Helen's reaction to Alison's declaration that she is lesbian is mediated through her father, as he writes, "Your mother's pretty upset though – not surprising" (Kron, 2015). It is important to remember that when Alison is reading that letter as a college student, she does not yet know her father is homosexual or that her mother knows of his homosexuality. She simply is lead to believe that her mother is falling into the expected stereotype of a parent who is shocked by the news her child is gay.

Not until "Days and Days," almost at the end of the play, does the audience gain any real insight into Helen or even recognize her as a fully drawn character. She laments, "… no one clocks the day you disappear." She feels her life has been, "… days of bargain I made because I thought as a wife I was meant to" (Kron, 2015). Helen acknowledges that she has rendered herself inconsequential because she thought it was what she was supposed to do. She believed that her role was to remain in the shadows and so she did. Her forced self-sacrifice may not have given Alison the support she needed as a child, but it is also provided an atmosphere which as a young adult did not judge her sexual identity or try to super-impose maternal desire. Helen's inconsequential parenting hurt herself, but in the long term allowed Alison to find her own voice.

To some degree, a similar claim can be made about the relationship between Evan and his mother Heidi in *Dear Evan Hanson*, the 2017 Tony Award winner for Best Musical. Written by Pasek and Paul, the composition team behind *La La Land*, *Dear Evan Hansen* is the story of social outcast Evan Hansen his chance encounter with another social outcast, Connor Murphy, just before his suicide. Due to a misunderstanding, Connor's family believes that Evan was Connor's only friend, and in his own desperate need to belong, Evan advances that fantasy, until he can no longer bear the burden of that lie and he confesses. The musical has gained enormous popularity, gaining a nearly cult following among teenagers, much like the *Netflix* series, *13 Reasons Why*, which also tackles teenage suicide and its aftermath.

In the first scene of *Dear Evan Hansen*, the audience meets Evan's mom, Heidi and Connor's mom, Cynthia, as both sing, "Does Anybody Have a Map?" Heidi asks, "So where's the map? / I need a clue / 'Cause the scary truth is / I'm flyin' blind / And I'm making this up as I go" (Pasek & Paul, 11). She is uncertain in her role as mother, struggling to find her relevance in her son's life. Cynthia too questions her own ability as a mother, stating, "I dunno if you can tell / But this is me just

/ Pretending to know" (Pasek & Paul, 13). Both mothers feel inept in their roles, unable to live up to the stereotypes set forth by society, but both longing, in some way to adhere to those expectations.

This longing is immediately profound for Cynthia, who reaches out in desperation to Evan just after her son, Connor's, death. Cynthia and her husband Larry approach Evan with what they think is Connor's suicide note. Cynthia rushes into this connection with Evan as a perceived replacement for her son. It begins the illusion, for Cynthia, that she mattered in her son's life and will matter in the life of this surrogate son. As the musical progresses, Cynthia's role is superficially more significant for Evan, as the illusion of her son's friendship also expands. To advance his own popularity, Evan also advances the illusion of the friendship. He paints the picture of the orchard, the place where Evan and Connor would go to talk, because it is what Cynthia needs to see. The image of the orchard is a substitute for the positive family life that Cynthia and Connor never shared. Instead of the mother creating the positive illusion for the child, here the roles are reversed and substituted. Evan creates the image of a loving space for his new mother figure. He is complicit in the image making, while she is oblivious, making her even more inconsequential than the audience first perceives.

As Cynthia's inconsequence becomes more evident to the audience, Heidi attempts to assert her relevance in Evan's life. Heidi works some nights and takes classes on others, but says to Evan, after she discovers that he may have known Connor, "Hey, you know what? How about I bag my shift next Tuesday? When's the last time we did a taco Tuesday?" (Pasek & Paul, 48). The conversation ends with "I love you" from both parties, which is genuine on both parts, but love and consequence are not equal. While mother and son do love each other, that love does not translate into significant daily interaction. Without such interaction, the two have been rendered inconsequential to each other. As Evan's interactions with Cynthia become more routine, Heidi senses the change in her son and tries to reclaim him.

This unspoken and even unconscious animosity crescendos when Zoe, Connor's sister, now Evan's girlfriend, invites Heidi to dinner at her family home, when Heidi and Cynthia meet for the first time. At this dinner, Heidi is embarrassed to learn that Evan has been spending most of his free time at the Murphy house. Cynthia and Larry offer to give Heidi the money from Connor's college savings account, and that is Heidi's breaking point. She defends herself; "No, no, I understand, I'm just, we do have money. So I'm sorry that you were under the impression that we didn't. And whatever money we don't have, Evan will either get a scholarship or he'll go to a community college and that's ... I think that's the best thing for us to do. I don't want Evan to get the idea that it's ok to rely on other people for favors" (Pasek & Paul, 131). She is asserting her dominance as his biological mother as she insists, "Well, but as his mother, I need to set that example for him. That you don't expect things from strangers" (Pasek & Paul, 131). Her language not only sets up an antithetical relationship between the two mother figures, but clearly asserts her dominance as the sole woman who is able to provide for her son. In asserting her own consequence in Evan's life, she diminishes the role of Cynthia as surrogate. This competition here is tremendously interesting as it posits biological mother again "adopted" one, but that adopted figure is only temporary and is born out of grief on the part of the mother and selfishness on the part of the son. Evan accepts Cynthia's motherly advances not only because he feels he lacks such tenderness from his own mother, but also because it helps him play the role of grieving friend, which he has assumed.

Cynthia needs Evan, as Connor's death, despite the fact that she has a living daughter, has undermined her own identity. In "Stabat Mater," Kristeva explains, "[A] mother's identity survives only thanks to the well-known fact that consciousness is lulled by habit, wherein a woman protects herself along the frontier that divides her body and makes an expatriate of her child. A kind of lucidity, however, might restore her, cut in tow, one half alien to the other – fertile soil for delirium. But also, and for that every reason maternity along its boarders destines us to experience a frenzied ecstasy to which by chance the nursling's laugh responds in the sunlit ocean's waters. What is the relationship between him and me? No relation, except that abundant laughter into which some sonorous, subtle, fluid identity collapses, gently carried by the waves" (146). In language meant to mirror the semiotic bond of mother and child, Kristeva's description of the experience of motherhood sheds light on Cynthia's position after her son's death. In the play's first scene, she falls into the habitual conversation she has had with Connor countless mornings before this one. The content of the words is nearly meaningless for her but the repetition of the pattern reinforces her motherly duty. That pattern, as it lulls her into a false sense of security, also temporarily protects her from seeing the pain her son is actually experiencing. That pattern has ironically put him at arms' length, and made her inconsequential in his life. His suicide becomes her lucid moment, but with him dead, she cannot restore that relationship and thus cannot reclaim her own identity, so she clings to Evan, a willing participant, to redefine herself. The orchard becomes the recreation of the idyll, which Kristeva characterizes of the sound of the infant's laughter.

When Evan finally confesses to Cynthia and Larry that he and Connor were not friends, and the letter was in fact, a letter he was writing to himself and not Connor's suicide note, Cynthia reacts in utter denial. After Evan's explanation, Cynthia simply walks off stage, with no ability to verbalize her feelings. Now, having lost two sons, she has nothing left, no identity to defend, and so she leaves the stage, inconsequential to herself.

In that moment, though, Evan's biological mother regains her importance, as if only one mother figure can exist for a child at one time. Evan's confession to the Murphy's morphs into a confession to Heidi. He cries, "You should [hate me]. If you knew what I tried to do. If you knew who I am, how. .. broken I am" (Pasek & Paul) and she responds, "I already know you. And I love you" (Pasek & Paul). There is both intense forgiveness and intense narcissism in her statement. Heidi knows her son in that he is biological part of her. Her love is a part of the transference which Lacan describes in the frame of the analyst. As Lacan explains, "... the positive transference is love" (*Four Fundamental Concepts*, 123). Transference, as we know from Freud, is the necessary relationship that analyst and analysand need to form for the analysis to be successful. In the analytic situation, as Freud rightly shows, the nature of that love, its authenticity, should be called into question. In the parental situation, the transference or the laying of one's own emotional state onto another is, in the best scenarios, the gift of true love, the shit which Derrida defines. Love, here, is Heidi's desire to move from inconsequential to consequential, so that she can take on and take over her son's pain. She promises him a life in which this huge pain will diminish and in the play's coda, it does. She steps forward only to step back again, this time, in tandem with her son's desire, so that he can find a way to survive. That is positive inconsequence.

An inconsequential state of motherhood can take several different forms. One can be inconsequential to one's self, which allows for little growth or freedom for the mother, and potentially not for the child unless radical steps are taken. The mother, in this state, has surrendered both her narcissistic bond to her child and her own narcissism.

Unless the mother beings a process of abjection through which she rids herself of all attachments, willfully, to develop and recognize a new self, such inconsequence does nothing but lead to emptiness. When a mother is inconsequential in the life of her child, the outcome had the potential to be far more positive. If that inconsequence is due to pure neglect, the child does not benefit, but if the mother actively chooses to step out of the child's life, to give the child room to develop his own sense of self, the consequences are positive. It seems though, that given the limited amount of musicals portraying these scenarios, which partially escape traditional stereotypes of motherhood that commercial audiences or producers are not ready to be challenged yet.

CHAPTER 5

The New Mother

Abstract This chapter will begin by looking at several examples of motherhood in contemporary Broadway that defy the categorizations of absent, overbearing, or inconsequential. *Caroline or Change* and *Next to Normal* give an alternate path of motherhood that may baffle the audience, but are productive for the mother figures. These are not traditional mothers, but their forms of mothering that offer freedom for the character and expand ways of thinking for the audience. After exploring these examples, this chapter will return to the theoretical premises of the introduction and offers suggestion for future productions.

Keywords Anagnorisis · Mirror stage · Symbolic

The closest Broadway musicals have come to real change or development in the idea, and portrayal of motherhood is exemplified in *Caroline, or Change* written by Tony Kushner with music by Jeanine Tesori. Perhaps because Kushner is a playwright by training, not a lyricist, that he is used to giving more thought to character development based in iconoclasm. Perhaps it is because Tesori is a woman, whose music reflects so many different styles, merging into one: spirituals, klezmer, Broadway, blues, and Motown that her score can reflect the different and competing elements alive in one figure. So many different mothers combined in one woman defy the usual mother figures already discussed.

© The Author(s) 2019
G. M. MacKenzie, *Maternal Representations in Twenty-First Century Broadway Musicals*, Pivotal Studies in the Global American Literary Imagination, https://doi.org/10.1007/978-3-030-32337-0_5

Caroline alternates among absent, overbearing, and inconsequential at different moments, but most of all, she is refreshingly loving and it is that love which allows her and her children, along with Noah, the boy for whom she stands as mother, to flourish.

Caroline, or Change is the story of a black maid in 1963 Lake Charles, Louisiana. Caroline is the maid to the Gellmans, a Jewish family consisting of father, Stuart, second wife, Rose, and 8-year-old Noah. Noah's mother died of cancer, and his father has remarried a woman who wants to do the best for her new husband and stepson but is faced with her own shortcomings. Caroline, the protagonist, is also the mother to three children; the oldest and only girl, Emmie is a rebel, wanting to fight for civil rights and frequently against her mother.

It seems easy to find instances of Caroline as the overbearing mother. At the beginning of the play, Noah sings, "Caroline who's always mad, / Caroline who runs everything, / Caroline who's stronger than my Dad" (Kushner, 2003). Noah imbues Caroline with traits more masculine than feminine, lending to her image as overbearing. The aggressive tendencies and rivalries that underlie the concept of the overbearing mother are also easily equated with masculinity. Since a strong father figure is missing from Noah's life, as his father is still devastated by his first wife's death, and since Caroline has had to be both mother and father to her children since her husband left, the overbearing aspects of her nature seem obvious. She is determined to find true strength, not just an overbearing overlay, in spite of her husband's abusive ways; she sings, "Let him see / He miss with me / After I have spent the day / Putting white folk's clothes away, / Tell him God, if he ever / ever / ever hit me again ..." (Kushner, 2003). She runs out of strength to finish her song, but her will has not expired. It has turned from being overbearing to being simply strong.

Such strength helps Caroline to know when she should be absent and when her absent is a detriment. After Rose begins to understand Caroline's financial difficulties and wants to teach Noah a lesson about responsibility, she tells Caroline that she can keep any change Noah leaves in his pockets. Caroline applies that rule when she finds a twenty-dollar bill in the laundry too that she desperately needs. After a raw, racially charged argument between Noah and Caroline, she leaves, not to return to work for five long days, during which Rose worries about Caroline and Noah struggles to hide the truth and come to terms with her being gone, as he sings repeatedly, " ... Caroline stayed away-way-way and she didn't come back back back and she didn't come back back back" finally ending with his lament, "I did it. I killed her. I did it she died" (Kushner, 2003).

It is not really Noah who is keeping Caroline away, as Mr. Stopnick, Rose's father explains. Rose, as stepmother, has forced Caroline's absence, even unconsciously, as her father points out, because she craves the maternal relationship with Noah that Caroline has. Her father helps her to see her own actions; "I don't mean you consciously planned to destroy in her Noah's affections – ... Well, not be design./ Maybe you had to– / One way or another / its hard, but not mean./ You got in between. / Maybe Rosie now you can be his mother" (Kushner, 2003). She retorts his assertions but sees the truth in them. Now, both of Noah's mothers, both biological and substitute ones, are absent. The effect on him is profound as he blames himself for their absences. In saying that he killed Caroline, he is expressing his fear that he, in some way, caused his mother's death and that he has the power to kill or at least drive others from him as well. That is a terrifying situation for an eight year old.

Meanwhile, in her absence, Caroline is also heartbroken, first that the boy she is raising can spew such racial hatred, and that she could spew it back, and second, that she truly misses the child she is effectually raising. In "Lot's Wife," she sings, "May madness rise up in a fury so wild and I let myself go. / Spoke my hate to a child" (Kushner, 2003). At the end of the lament prompted by her grief for Noah, she fiercely embraces her own daughter, with whom she has been struggling. The differences in their opinions on race relations and financial matters have separated them, making Caroline nearly functionally absent in Emmie's life, but she needs to be a mother and so the embrace is not just about her love for her daughter, which it is, in part, but also about her embracing her life as a mother. She will return to her job, earn money, albeit very little money, to support her own children and be the supportive maternal figure Noah needs. She will end the absence that has put a strain on all their lives.

Caroline may have been absent either functionally, or physically at some points, but she has never been inconsequential. She only believes herself to be. When she laments about money and her inability to give her children what they need, she articulates her own perceived inadequacy. She begs, of the universe, in "Ironing," Please give me a mop and bucket. / Please, a white folks house to tend. / Please some money, feed the babies" (Kushner, 2003). She wants to work, to be relevant in the lives of her children, to be able to work to provide for them, but she fears that she will lose the ability to do that, and that even with a job, she will not be able to care for her children's basic needs. Caroline would be content to be inconsequential to the world, as long as she could be useful to her children, but Emmie is not happy with her mother's choices. At the Gellman's party, she screams at her mother, "You tippy-toe till you been paid. / You the spoiled one! A maid! / I'll never be a queen, that's true, / But I'm a damn sight better'n prouder'n you! / Come on, teach me what you know! / Mama teach me what you know! / How to keep my head tucked low. / Come on, come one / Teach me what you know!" (Kushner, 2003). She is begging for her mother not to be inconsequential; Emmie wants Caroline to see herself as important and significant in the world, because that is what Emmie herself wants to be. "Lot's Wife" shows the audience that Caroline does not want to be of greater importance in the world. She would be happy to be more significant in her daughter's life, and the embrace they share at the end of the song shows that. That embrace is also tacit permission that Caroline gives to Emmie to be bigger than she has ever been or wants to be. In "Epilogue," Emmie stands on stage alone, after Caroline leaves her in the early morning light, to assume her own power. She will become who she is destined to be because of her mother's choice to stay on in the shadows. Emmie asserts, "I am the daughter of a maid, / In her uniform, crisp and clean! / Nothing can ever make me afraid!" (Kushner, 2003). She repeats, "I am the daughter of a maid. / She stands alone where the harsh winds blow: / Salting the Earth so nothing grow / Too close; but still her strong blood flow ... / Under ground through hidden veins, / Down from storm clouds when it rains, / Down the plains, down the high plateau / Down to the Gulf of Mexico. / Down to Larry and Emmie and Jackie and Joe. / The children of Caroline Thibodeaux" (Kushner, 2003). Emmie will pursue a life of rebellion against the racism, classism, and sexism that her mother will not resist, but she can only do that because her mother chose not to. Caroline has been inconsequential in the eyes of the world. She is unremarkable in every way, but her lack of consequence has empowered her daughter.

Caroline is the best example twenty-first-century Broadway musicals offer of a mother who defies convention. In the face of every prejudice a woman in 1963 American could face, she makes her own choices. They are not the choices that her family wants her to make, nor are they the choices that audience hopes for, for her, but they are the correct ones for her. In her choices, Caroline is able to do what makes her most comfortable and what will help her children to grow.

The outcome is positive for all parties involved. A happy ending though, one that looks forward to a more free or generative future is not necessary. What is needed is great depth and opportunity for mother figures to be developed in musical theatre.

The dramatic stage does this and has done this for decades, with brilliance. The great psychological dramas of Eugene O'Neil, written and staged long before the Golden Age of musical theatre, the dazzlingly painful maternal relationships staged, and underlying the works of Tennessee Williams, the quietly obstinate mothers of Arthur Miller each give more fully drawn characters, with greater range than nearly any musical mother figure, even those analyzed here. In much more recent Broadway history, plays such as *God of Carnage*, *Rabbit Hole*, and *August, Osage County* have given great range and opportunity for highly nuanced mother figures with complex relationships to their statuses as mothers. These plays have all been both critically and commercially successful, so if drama can do it, why can't musical theatre? At least, why hasn't musical theatre been able to do it to a great extent yet?

The answer to that question lies in part, to the history and form of musical theatre itself. Musical theatre has a rather proscribed form, even when acting against type. There are two acts, generally, with only a few shows, notably by Weber and Sondheim, that have "intermission" problems, or no strictly definable mid-point in the narrative. What nearly all commercially produced musical have in common are the following elements: the "ask," the conditional "love" song, the second couple, the villains, the subplot, the "candy dish," the climax, and "next to last" and the conclusion. These elements are all based on the structure that Jack Viertel outlines in *The Secret Life of the American Musical*. Each of these conventions drives the musical to a usually happy, romantic conclusion. As Viertel points out, specifically about *Bloody Bloody Andrew Jackson*, and *Passing Strange*, " … there failure to find large, appreciative audiences has a lot to do with their formlessness" (5). Musical theatre audiences have been trained to expect a certain shape and content; when that shape shifts, audiences have difficulty understanding how to appreciate what they are watching. For a musical such as *Passing Strange*, when both form is already defying expectation, to have characters also written against type, the outcome is a commercial death sentence.

To again use *Passing Strange* and Viertel as explanation, the Broadway musical is "supposed" to be a love story or at least a story to entice romantic feelings. Viertel explains,

> [M]ost musical are romances and for decades the principal responsibility of the Broadway musical was to be effective aphrodisiac. What is a night out, after all, if not an invitation to intimacy? And if the songs, heard later in a club or on a bedside radio, cause a revival of passionate feelings, so much better. This may sound like a trivial pursuit for an art form, but it's just the opposite. The Broadway musical, in its heyday, was an integral part of human courtship for a considerable, portion of the American population. It gave validity to the idea of taking sex seriously, while laughing at it, along with those of us who were perpetually trying to figure out romantic love. It showed us beautiful, sensuous, sinuous people trying to get it right, which inspired the rest of us mere mortals to redouble our efforts. It gave harmonic voice to desire and ecstasy in ways we never dared to do out loud in our own lives. And it endorsed the idea that romance – the kind that demands a bed right away – far from being destructive, was the first building block to happiness in society. That was very encouraging. (8–9)

Moving from that brilliantly sketched analysis, of musicals in the Golden Age and beyond, Viertel traces the history of changes to the musical, in terms of structure and musical style, citing stunningly successful and less than successful experiments, such as *A Chorus Line, Urinetown, Les Miserables,* and *Hamilton.* No doubt those and other have dazzled audiences, and for good reasons, but none of the examples Viertel explores to explain the developments to the commercial musical address significantly different characterization in general or the development of the mother figure specifically.

The development of the mother figure in ways more significant than secondary or stereotypical is counterintuitive to an evening of romance that begins with a ticket to a Broadway show. The assumption, accurate for many, is that watching a parental angst does not typically entice feelings of sexual desire, and since sex still sells, shows that offer romance or at least escapism in the same vein that romance might have the biggest box office draws.

The problem is that Broadway audiences are changing. Individuals cannot afford to buy tickets to a musical every time they want to seduce or be seduced. Now, they swipe right to Netflix and chill. The market is changing. Refreshingly, after years of hearing that "Broadway is dead" and the audiences are only filled with rich white folks, the audiences are starting to change, as is the content. First humor in musical theatre attracted new audience members. Shows such as *Spamalot* and *The Book of Mormon*, written by widely known and respected comedians, have helped make great strides in attracting atypical audience members. The Disney revolution on Broadway has brought families back to the theatre and reinvigorated interest, which is staying with those young audience members as they mature. *Rent* and *Avenue Q* help to keep young adults interested after their Disney days have passed. All the musicals discussed in this text have great appeal for this new generation of theatregoer, the teenager/young adult, looking to connect with media and story beyond social media platforms. This age group is mired in parental struggles; issues concerning mothers and motherhood effect their daily lives. They need to see those same issues reflected on stage, or they will lose interest.

Yes, there are other ways to connect with this age group. *Hamilton* is a phenomenal success in part because Lin-Manuel Miranda is able to integrate not only the hip-hop sound, but the sensibilities that accompany that sound, to the Broadway stage. That has certainly attracted a younger audience, in a musical that has very little to do with mother/child storylines. After all, Hamilton's mother dies when he is young and the musical frames Hamilton's lifelong nemesis as Aaron Burr, not the psychological scars of being orphaned. Still, *Hamilton*'s ability to transcend and connect is a brilliant anomaly.

Musical theatre needs more accurate and widely ranging depictions of mothers and motherhood. To do this, the art form needs its own moment of anagnorisis. In *Poetics*, Aristotle asserts that the two most necessary components of tragedy are anagnorisis and peripeteia or recognition and reversal. Aristotle strictly referred to the recognition of the hero of his true nature and fate. Oedipus's anagnorisis is that he has murdered and father and married his mother, despite her efforts to thwart his fate. Anagnorisis in Greek tragedy is a mechanism for catharsis. If the hero acknowledges some universal truth, again, as in *Oedipus Rex*, that one cannot escape his fate, then the audience can learn via secondhand experience, and not make the same error.

While most commercially successful musicals are not true tragedies, many of tragic elements. The end of *Gypsy*, in its different iterations and stagings, usually leaves Rose with a quiet recognition of her mistakes. Regardless of final tableau presented, the last song of the musical is "Rose's Turn," during which she questions her life choices and how those have led to her own personal demise. She bears all to the audience articulating her regrets, and the dreams that she has never let herself dream for herself. She realizes all she has done has backfired. The musical may not be strictly Aristotelean in approach, but it is tragic. Rose recognizes her failures and, in some versions, works to reverse her relationship with Louise.

There are, among those musicals already discussed, other outstanding examples of anagnorisis. Diana in *Next to Normal* has both sweeping and shocking recognition of herself. When she leaves her husband and daughter at the end of Act 2, it is because she sees that she cannot change her essential nature and is not willing to give up her relationship with her son. She refuses the reversal required of Aristotelean tragedy. She will not abandon the fantasy she has built around Gabe, but she recognizes her unwillingness to do so and acts to maintain that fantasy, while attempting to give her living family a chance for a more "normal" life. In other musicals explored already, it is the daughter who experiences the anagnorisis. Alison, in *Fun Home*, sees the truth about her family and herself. By the end of the musical, she is comfortable living as a lesbian; she understands that her father hid his sexual identity from her and that her mother was complicit in this deceit. There is no reversal necessary, unless turning back time is an option. Emmie in *Caroline, or Change* is another example of a daughter who sees the truth of hers and her mother's lives. While Emmie is the brutal voice of truth for her mother throughout *Caroline, or Change*, in "Epilogue," she finally is able to see that her budding freedom and activism are because of her mother, as she sings, "I'm the daughter of a maid. / She stands alone where the harsh winds blow: / Salting the Earth so nothing grow / Too close; but still her strong blood flow..." (Kushner, 2015). What Emmie has seen in Caroline fuels her own passions.

In *Spring Awakening*, the recognition does not come from either mother or daughter figures, but from the son/lover left behind. Melchior, the only main character left alive in this nearly Shakespearean tragedy, sees how flawed parental relationships have destroyed his generation. He has recognized the destruction that he has witnessed and been a part of, yet, he promises to move forward the dreams of those whose lives have been wasted.

To be operative in more musical theatre productions concerning mother/child relationships, there also has to be an understanding of how anagnorisis might work within that dyad. For such understanding,

Lacan begins to offer some insight. The mirror stage is the quintessential moment of anagnorisis. When the child recognizes that she is being held by her mother in the mirror and that the reflection does not show a separate or independent being, the child's erroneous claim to autonomy is shattered. For Lacan's taxonomy, this is the movement from the Imaginary to the Symbolic stages. In the Imaginary, the child believes she has control and autonomy. In the Symbolic, she realizes that such independence is an illusion. As Lacan explains, "[T]he moment at which the mirror stage comes to an end inaugurates, through identification with the image of one's semblable and the drama of primordial jealousy … It is this moment that decisively tips the whole of human knowledge [*savior*] into being mediated by the other's desire, constitutes its objects in an abstract equivalence due to competition from other people, and turn the *I* into an aperture to which every instinctual pressure constitutes danger, even if it corresponds to a natural maturation process" (7). With the recognition that one needs support comes the understanding that such support comes at the price of oneself. Lacan doesn't talk about the obverse effect on the mother who is recently discovered as needed and resented for that role. Kristeva fills in that gap with the concept of the abject as the mother sees her child in the material that both she and her child expel.

That material should be the material that is staged more often in commercial musical theatre. Each audience member has been through the process, whether as mother, child, or both. So much intimacy already exists with the process that is difficult to write, to embrace, and to market, but it is necessary. The mother/child dyad lies at the heart of human experience. Musical theatre can uniquely sing that experience and should with great range. Without expanding its range, musical theatre risks great loss, as audiences need more than what they are being given. They don't need the date night anymore; they need the reality of the morning after or lifetime after.

They also need to see a new kind of mother figure, and their parents need to see that figure as well. Here, the term figure, singular, is actually a misnomer, as the singular figure is not what is needed. What is needed is a multiplicity of figures to populate the stage or stages of commercial musical theatre, so that variety that reflects actual human experience is showcased. Lacan famously writes, "[T]here's no such thing as Woman, Woman with a capital *W* indicating the universal. There's no such thing as Woman because, in her essence – I've already risked using that term, so why should I think twice about using it again? – she is not-whole" (*On Feminine Sexuality*, 72–73). Lacan is easily criticized for this statement, but it is not a negative commentary. It makes the claim that woman is a category, but women are uncharacterizable; " ... there is always something in her that escapes discourse" (*On Feminine Sexuality*, 33). The escape, the slippage between what can be seen and what lies underneath, helps to explain why women cannot be limited. That which slips under, around, or beside the stereotype is the true essence of what any one woman might be. In her introduction to *Feminine Sexuality*, Jacqueline Rose explains, "[W]hat this means is that femininity is assigned to a point of origin prior to the mark of symbolic difference and the law. The privileged relationship of women to that origin gives them access to an archaic form of expressivity outside the circuit of linguistic exchange" (54). That means that women can communicate beyond the confines of language codes; as Cixous explained, women can write the body for themselves. Women characters, of course, are not writing themselves, but as they are being written with as much truth as possible, women characters seem particularly suited for musical theatre, which conveys its plot and character through so much more than words or dialogue. It seems the musical is an ideally suited art form for the development of women characters.

To develop completely the woman on the Broadway musical stage, motherhood must be explored in all its potential facets. That means the creation of new figures, not categories, but individual figures who are able to transcend the bonds of maternity, while still representing it. Rose writes of motherhood in general, "[T]he duality of the relation between mother and child must be broken" (*Feminine Sexuality*, 38), and so it must; the duality can no longer be the defining characteristic of motherhood. Instead, like the category of "Woman," "Mother" cannot longer be a category. Instead, we need mothers of all types, to give a more full range of representation.

BIBLIOGRAPHY

Beguelin, Chad, and Matthew Sklar. *The Prom*. Masterworks Broadway, 2018.

Boubil, Alain, and Claude-Michel Schonberg. Trans. Herbert Kretzmer. *Les Miserable (The Original London Cast Recording)*. First Night, 2012.

Caldwell, Lesley, Ed. *Winnicott and the Psychoanalytic Tradition*. London: Karnac, 2008.

Duplessis, Rachel Blau. *Writing Beyond the Ending: Narrative Strategies of Twentieth Century Women Writers*. Bloomington: Indiana University Press, 1985.

Finn, William. *The 25th Annual Putnam Country Spelling Bee*. SH-K Boom Records, Inc., 2005.

Hall, Lee, and Elton John. *Billy Elliot: The Musical*. Verve, 2005.

Kantor, Michael, and Laurence Maslon. *Broadway: An American Musical*. New York: Applause, 2010.

Klein, Melanie, and Joan Riviere. *Love, Hate and Reparation*. London: W. W. Norton, 1964. Print.

Knapp, Raymond. *The American Musical and the Performance of Personal Identity*. Princeton: Princeton University Press, 2006. Print.

Kristeva, Julia. Ed. Leon S. Roudiez. *Desire in Language: A Semiotic Approach to Literature and Art*. New York: Columbia University Press, 1980.

Kristeva, Julia. Ed. Leon S. Roudiez. *Powers of Horror: An Essay on Abjection*. New York: Columbia University Press, 1982.

Kristeva, Julia. Stabat Mater. *Poetics Today*. Vol. 6: 1–2 (1985), 133–152.

Kron, Lisa, and Jeanine Tesori. *Fun Home*. PS Classics, 2015.

Kushner, Tony, and Jeanine Tesori. *Caroline, or Change*. Hollywood, 2004.

© The Editor(s) (if applicable) and The Author(s), under exclusive license to Springer Nature Switzerland AG 2019
G. M. MacKenzie, *Maternal Representations in Twenty-First Century Broadway Musicals*, Pivotal Studies in the Global American Literary Imagination, https://doi.org/10.1007/978-3-030-32337-0

Lacan, Jacques. Trans. Alan Sheridan. *The Seminar of Jacques Lacan: The Four Fundamental Concepts of Psychoanalysis.* New York: W. W. Norton, 1981.

Lacan, Jacques. Trans. Jacqueline Rose. *Feminine Sexuality.* New York: W. W. Norton, 1985.

Lacan, Jacques. Ed. Jacques-Alain Miller. Trans. Bruce Fink. *On Feminine Sexuality: The Limits of Love And Knowledge, 1972–1973.* New York: W. W. Norton, 1988.

Lacan, Jacques. Trans. Bruce Fink. *Ecrits.* New York: W. W. Norton, 2002.

McMillin, Scott. *The Musical as Drama.* Princeton: Princeton University Press, 2006.

Minchin, Tim. *Matilda: The Musical.* Broadway Records. Yellow Sound Labe, 2013.

Mordden, Ethan. *On Sondheim: An Opinionated Guide.* New York: Oxford University Press, 2016.

Morel, Geneveive. Trans. Lindsay Watson. *The Low of the Mother: An Essay on the Sexual Sinthome.* New York: Routledge, 2019.

Pasek, Benj, and Justin Paul. *Dear Evan Hansen.* Atlantic Records, 2017.

Rose, Jacqueline. *Mothers: An Essay on Love and Cruelty.* New York: Farrar, Strauss, and Giroux, 2018.

Rudnytsky, Peter. L. Ed. *Transitional Objects and Potential Spaces: Literary Uses of D. W. Winnicott.* New York: Columbia University Press, 1993.

Russell, Brenda, Allee Willi, and Stephen Bray. *The Color Purple: A New Musical.* Angel Records. 2005.

Sater, Steven, and Duncan Sheik. *Spring Awakening.* Verve, 2006.

Schwartz, Stephen. *Wicked.* Verve, 2003.

Secrest, Meryle. *Stephen Sondheim: A Life.* New York: Random House, 1998.

Sellers, Susan, et al. *The Helene Cixous Reader.* New York: Routledge, 1994.

Sondheim, Stephen, and Jules Styne. *Gypsy (2008 Broadway Cast Recording).* Time Life/WEA, 2008.

Sondheim, Stephen. *Into the Woods (Original Cast Recording).* Masterworks Broadway, 2011.

Sondheim, Stephen. *Into the Woods.* Masterworks, 2007.

Stew, and Heidi Rodewald. *Passing Strange: The Complete Book and Lyrics of the Broadway Musical by Stew.* New York: Applause, 2009.

Viertel, Jack. *The Secret Life of the American Musical: How Broadway Shows are Built.* New York: Farrar, Straus and Giroux, 2016. Print.

Winnicott, D. W. *Playing and Reality.* New York: Routledge, 1989.

Wolf, Stacy Ellen. *Changed for Good: A Feminist History of the Broadway Musical.* New York: Oxford University Press, 2011.

Yorkey, Brian, and Tom Kitt. *Next to Normal.* Ghostlight Records, 2009.

INDEX

CPSIA information can be obtained
at www.ICGtesting.com
Printed in the USA
LVHW041849011219
639064LV00014B/898/P